PETA FILES

The Dark Side of the Animal Rights Movement

Dave Workman

Merril Press
Bellevue, Washington

8-5-04

First Edition
February 2003

Merril Press
Merril Mail Marketing Inc.
P O Box 1682
Bellevue, WA 98009
425-454-7009
Visit out website for additional copies ($15.00 each) of this
title and others at www.merrilpress.com

Cover Photo © Eagle Stock Images

Library of Congress Cataloging-In-Publication Data

Workman, Dave P., 1949-
  PETA files : the darks side of the animal rights movement /
Dave Workman. – 1st ed.
      p. cm.
  Includes bibliographical references.
  ISBN 0-936783-32-X
People for the Ethical Treatment of Animals. 2. Animal rights
movement—Moral and ethical aspects—United States. 3.
Animal welfare—Moral and ethical aspects—United States.
I. Title.

HV4763.W67 2003
179'.3'0973—dc21
          2003042175

Printed in the United States of America

DEDICATION

For my family – Dacey, Rhett and Josh. And for my
hunting partners, who are part of my extended family.

It is not how much time we have, but how we use it
and who we choose to spend it with.

TABLE OF CONTENTS

One

MONEY TO BURN

Ka-*whoomp!*

The blaze erupted with that unmistakable sound one hears when a ball of fire consumes every bit of oxygen in the immediate area, and the air is sucked out of that space to be replaced by a blistering rush of heat and burst of yellow, white and orange light. It was that sudden "whoosh" one hears when someone throws a cup of gasoline on an open flame.

Ignited by the detonation of what the authorities would later call "a timed incendiary device," and would also be alternately described as a "fire bomb" in published reports, the devastating blaze was soon acknowledged to be something else: a deliberate, unprovoked attack on the Oregon State University's mink farm in Corvallis. Loss due to damages came to $75,000.

That damage included what happened at mink farm research offices nearby, which were vandalized and burglarized. The perpetrators of this crime were not shy about leaving what would become, over the next 16 months, a familiar greeting: spray-painted threats on the walls, and calls or news releases to local television and radio stations and the Associated Press.

This was not the work of some crazy fanatics from the Middle East, but a group of home-grown extremists whose three-letter acronym was already well-known in the outdoors community and would become the focus for a multi-state law enforcement investigation: ALF – the Animal Liberation Front.

Authorities could not know it at the time, but the June 10, 1991 arson at OSU was the opening assault of what ALF called "Operation Bite Back," an aggressive, destructive campaign against fur farming and medical research; a sort of "wake up call" over ten years prior to the attacks of Sept. 11, 2001 that made it clear not all terrorists come from some foreign land.

This was not the first time ALF had made headlines. The loosely-knit radical group had been active in the United States since the late 1970s, having first appeared in Great Britain a few years before.

It was also not the first time ALF had made news in Oregon. Almost five years earlier, in October 1986, an elementary school teacher in Portland named Roger Troen "became involved" in an animal rights "liberation" effort mounted against the University of Oregon at Eugene. According to various published reports, Troen – identified as "a known animal advocate" in an issue of *No Compromise*, an animal rights newsletter – allegedly received what he claimed was an anonymous phone call from someone asking him to drive to Eugene and "take some animals in desperate need of a home." Translation: He was invited to help steal the animals, which were later identified by the *Portland Oregonian* as 100 rats, 30 mice, 11 hamsters and three rabbits.

Troen's mistake was in having the animals examined by a veterinarian, who turned him in to the police after discovering University of Oregon tattoos on the stolen rabbits. At the time, the animals were being kept at the home of a friend of Troen's on the Oregon coast. In January 1988, Troen was convicted on charges of first-degree theft and second degree burglary, drawing a 6-month home detention sentence and a fine of $34,900, and five years probation.

Charges in connection with this raid were dropped against three other men, including one identified as Jonathan Paul, an animal rights activist who would later become involved in protests against Makah tribal whaling activities near Neah Bay, Washington.

According to testimony before the House Resources Committee, Subcommittee on Forests and Forest Health on Feb. 12, 2002 by James F. Jarboe, Domestic Terrorism Section Chief with the Counterterrorism division of the Federal Bureau of Investigation, ALF members have been a busy bunch. Typically, Jarboe stated, these radicals have been taking "direct action" against specific targets, "…in the form of criminal activity to cause economic loss or to destroy the victims' company operations."

That just about sums up the June 10 attack in Corvallis. According to court documents, witnesses in Corvallis "recalled seeing a female and a male similar in appearance" to a man who would later become the object of an intense nationwide manhunt, and who would be directly linked with Operation Bite Back. His name was Rodney Adam Coronado, arguably one of the most active, and dangerous, animal rights extremists in the United States.

A Yaqui Indian, Coronado has been described in court documents – specifically a sentencing report filed in the U.S. District Court for the Western District of Michigan, Southern Division – as "a long-time advocate of the rights of animals." He joined the Sea Shepherd Conservation Society, an off-shoot of the environmental group Greenpeace, in 1984. Sea Shepherd extremists were involved in a series of attacks on the commercial fishing industry by sabotaging fishing nets.

At that time, and even today, the particular nets attacked by Sea Shepherd raiders were not terribly popular. Known as drift nets, and described in sport fishing publications as "walls of death," they could stretch for miles and ensnare everything in their paths. If abandoned, they simply continued killing for years because the rotted and decaying corpses of the fish and marine mammals caught in them would make way for fresh victims. If the nets sank under the weight of the dead marine life, they would eventually resurface when the bodies of the victims had been devoured or simply fallen away from the nylon mesh. These nets were primarily the tools of renegade Asian fishing vessels, operating in the northern Pacific and often illegally inside United States territorial waters.

These outlaw fishermen were blamed with helping to decimate salmon and steelhead runs in Alaska, Canada and the Pacific Northwest. Because of this, many in the sport fishing and outdoors community did not show much dismay over net-cutting attacks.

But Coronado was a cut above some of his colleagues in the Sea Shepherd Society in terms of devotion, which is no doubt why his name would become synonymous with animal rights terrorism in the 1990s, and be directly associated with Operation Bite Back. By that time, he had become a legend in the animal rights terrorist community.

In 1986, Coronado accompanied Paul Watson, captain of the *Sea Shepherd*, to Reykjavik, Iceland, where they sabotaged a whaling station and sank two whaling vessels, according to the federal court document, and Watson's own admission.

Months later, he surfaced with a new cause and became first associated with ALF when he vandalized nine fur salons in Vancouver, Canada. He and several others "smashed windows and spray painted slogans such as 'Fur is Deadly' and 'ALF' at the businesses," said the Michigan court report.

In 1990 under the alias "Jim Perez," Coronado was in Hamilton, Montana at the Huggans Rocky Mountain Fur Farm, where he made a photocopy of a list of all the fur breeders in the Pacific Northwest. This list included their addresses.

Five days after the OSU arson, the Northwest Farm Food Cooperative in Edmonds, Washington, located about halfway between Seattle and Everett on Puget Sound, was firebombed. It made big headlines in Seattle and Everett newspapers, and forever put ALF on the landscape in the Pacific Northwest.

NWFFC's crime, at least in the eyes of the ALF terrorists, was that it was a food supply house for fur breeders, especially in Washington and Oregon.

There was another significant reason that NWFFC was targeted: Its association with Oregon State University's mink farm operation. The burglary of OSU's mink farm offices could easily have turned up paperwork linking the university with the feed supply.

Investigators at the two fires learned that the same type of "incendiary device" had been used to start both arsons.

If there was any doubt about a connection between the fires, it evaporated when ALF issued a press release taking credit for the Edmonds fire, and stating that the arson was committed because of the ties between the two facilities. If anyone thought that the two attacks were all the "bite" in Operation Bite Back, they would soon learn that they were mistaken.

After all, they needed only to refer to the communiqué that had been issued by ALF while the OSU fire was actually still smoldering. It said, in part, that ALF raids would continue "with similar actions until the last fur farm is burned to the ground."

August Offensive

Two months passed as investigators continued combing through the ashes in Oregon and Washington. Then, on Aug. 1, Coronado, again using the alias "Jim Perez," released a press statement on behalf of an organization calling itself the "Coalition Against Fur Farms" in which he detailed the June ALF raids and claimed they were "crimes of compassion."

During this period Coronado, accompanied by two females, had been staying in the southeastern Washington college town of Pullman. This community, located in the rolling Palouse Hills wheat farming region, is home to Washington State University, whose reputation for work in agriculture and livestock, veterinary medicine and other animal-related fields is renowned. Coronado and his companions were in Pullman, according to the Michigan court report, "house sitting."

True enough, as it turns out. According to court documents from the federal 9th Circuit Court of Appeals in San Francisco, Coronado occupied the Pullman home of James Richard Scarce, a PhD student at WSU's Department of Sociology, and the author of various essays on the environmental and animal rights movement, and the book, *Eco-Warriors: Understanding the Radical Environmental Movement* (Noble Press 1990) which detailed Coronado's activities. Coronado stayed at Scarce's house while Scarce and his family were on vacation, from mid-July through Aug. 14, 1991.

On the night of Aug. 12, a fur animal research facility at WSU was vandalized and burglarized, though the damage was nowhere near that suffered at OSU and the Edmonds feed plant. The burglary in WSU's Bustad Hall netted the release of ten mice, seven coyotes and a single mink, along with what one report called "substantial damage" to documents and fixtures. In fact, the perpetrators spread hydrochloric acid throughout the laboratories, causing approximately $100,000 in damages.

After the attack, an ALF press release took credit and announced that future attacks were coming. That communiqué specifically threatened the safety of six individuals: Davis Prieur, John Gorham, Fred Gilbert, David Shen, William Foreyt and Mark Robinson. The threat was clear: "Until coyotes, and other animals live free from the torturous (sic) hand of humankind, no industry or individual is safe from the rising tide of fur animal liberation...ALF is watching and there is no place to hide."

The six threatened people were all scientists involved in animal research.

When Scarce returned to the Pullman airport the evening of Aug. 14, Coronado was there to meet the plane. He drove them home. The next morning, according to court documents, Coronado had breakfast with Scarce and his wife, Petra Uhrig, at which time they discussed a story in the local newspaper about the WSU vandalism.

Later called before a grand jury to answer questions about Coronado's stay at his home, Scarce refused to cooperate, declining to answer on the grounds that he was entitled to a "scholar's privilege" under the First Amendment and common law. On April 6, 1993, the federal district court rejected that argument, and the 9th Circuit Court affirmed that ruling on May 6, 1993, holding Scarce in contempt.

In the aftermath of the Pullman raid, according to the Michigan court document, Coronado was interviewed (anonymously) by a Portland television station, KGW, in which he identified himself as "no stranger to the Animal Liberation Front," and further acknowledged that he had participated in the WSU attack. He also vowed further violations of the law.

Sixteen days elapsed before the next ALF attack, and this one was hundreds of miles away. On Aug. 28, there was an attempted arson at the Fur Breeders Agriculture Co-op in Sandy, Utah. As ALF attacks go, this one did not amount to much because the incendiary device did not go off as designed. That was a stroke of luck for investigators because now they had a complete firebomb to study.

The Utah raid had one other earmark of an ALF action: graffiti. Surprisingly, though, there was no press release to publicize the event, perhaps because the firebomb did not detonate. (ALF would return six years later, on March 11, 1997, to set four firebombs in the Agricultural Fur Breeders facility, causing an estimated $1 million in damage.)

Following the Aug. 28 attack, ALF went quiet again, for nearly four months.

On the night of Dec. 12, 1991, someone attempted to burglarize the Huggans Rocky Mountain Fur Farm. The perpetrators were surprised, however, and they fled before doing any serious harm. But fur was definitely on the minds of the would-be burglars, because nine days later, and two states away, another fur producer was targeted.

Sometime during the night of Dec. 21-22, 1991, the Malecky Mink Ranch in Yamhill, Oregon which works with OSU on projects related to mink breeding and nutrition, was burned to the ground. Later that night, an anonymous male called Portland's KGW, claiming to be an ALF member and taking credit for the Malecky Farm arson. Telephone records discovered during the investigation indicated that Coronado had placed that telephone call. About six weeks later, in the Feb. 2, 1992 issue of *Earth First! Journal*, ALF again took credit for the Yamhill attack.

More than two months elapsed following the Dec. 21 attack and the next raid, perhaps the most destructive of all. A week before Michigan State University in East Lansing was the target of a massive arson, burglary and vandalism on the night of Feb. 28, 1992, Coronado – this time accompanied by two women identified as Deborah Stout and Kimberly Trimiew – arrived in Michigan, according to court records. The night before the MSU attack, Coronado and Stout checked into an Ann Arbor hotel.

This particular incident was to earn the focus of not only criminal investigators, but organizations whose interests had been long targeted and criticized by the overall animal rights movement. This time, as in two earlier events in 1989, when ALF publicized its responsibility for the attack, its press release was not sent out from a commercial copying center as was Coronado's typical *modus operandi*.

This time, the release was issued by an organization well known to hunters, ranchers, trappers, circuses and furriers: People for the Ethical Treatment of Animals, known by the acronym PETA.

How Closely Tied?

Considered the largest animal rights organization in the world, PETA was founded in 1980 by Ingrid Ward Newkirk and Alex Pacheco, and is currently based in Norfolk, Virginia, having moved there from Silver Spring, Maryland. There are also offices in Europe, and PETA has gained a reputation for fur protests here, in Europe and Hong Kong.

There are various accounts about how PETA became a reality, and depending upon which account one accepts as gospel, the organization was Pacheco's brain-child, and Newkirk helped make the dream a reality.

Pacheco was raised in Mexico and Ohio, graduating from high school there and attending Ohio State University with the goal of becoming a Catholic priest. All of that changed in 1978 when he was visiting a friend in Toronto and they went to a slaughterhouse, hardly what one would consider a stop on the "A-Tour" during any normal description of a vacation. What Pacheco saw there made him physically ill and he reportedly became a vegetarian from that moment forward. The transformation into animal rights activist was solidified when he read a copy of *Animal Liberation* by Peter Singer, met with some animal rights activists and, in the summer of 1979, traveled aboard the *Sea Shepherd* to Europe, where he would become involved – apparently as an onlooker and photographer – in the ramming of the whaling ship *Sierra* by the *Sea Shepherd* in July of that year in Portuguese waters. The *Sea Shepherd* was, of course, the "flagship" of the Sea Shepherd Society, which would – five years after Pacheco climbed aboard – attract Rodney Coronado to her decks.

Animal Liberation, first published in 1975, is considered by many to be the manifesto of the modern animal rights movement, and Singer the movement's "godfather." Singer, a native of Australia, is a professor of bioethics, and has taught at several American universities. He is also author to several books other than *Animal Liberation*, including several books he co-authored with others who are involved in animal rights and environmental politics.

Among the more controversial of Singer's books is *Should the Baby Live? The Problem of Handicapped Infants (Studies in Bioethics)*, co-authored with Helga Kuhse. Singer is no wallflower when it comes to the subject of killing babies. By his own statements, he seems far more at ease with the killing of infant children than he does with the prospect of killing animals. At the 2002 Animal Rights Conference in McLean, Virginia, Singer – an avowed atheist – discussed his view that a severely handicapped infant could be killed within a month of its birth, "if the parents deem the baby's life is not worth living," according to an account that appeared on CNSNews.com, July 2, 2002.

The controversial academic further explained to CNSNews' Mark Morano: "If you have a being that is not sentient, that is not even aware, then the killing of that being is not something that is wrong in and of itself."

Another of Singer's books, *Practical Ethics*, is reportedly one of the most widely used texts in courses on ethics currently taught on university campuses.

Singer remains one of the most influential animal rights spokespersons, and he suggested that Christianity is "a problem" for that movement, no doubt because of Biblical teachings that man shall have dominion over the Earth and all its other creatures. This philosophy is what Singer has branded as "speciesism," defined as giving one species – humans – the belief that it is superior to all other species. Both Singer's writing and his philosophy left a lasting impression on the impressionable Pacheco.

Almost immediately after the *Sea Shepherd* incident, Pacheco beat a hasty path to England, where, according to various biographies, he joined the Hunt Saboteurs Association. That group was organized to interfere with traditional English fox hunts.

When he returned from England, Pacheco transferred to George Washington University and gave up all thoughts about the priesthood, apparently, choosing instead to study political science as his major.

Newkirk's background is even more curious, considering some of the things she has done that have gotten her on the wrong side of the law. A native of England, where she was born in Surrey in 1949, she was raised in a family that always had pets. Her father's occupation took them to India, where – according to author Ron Arnold in his book

EcoTerror – she witnessed for the first time acts of cruelty to animals.

She came to the United States with her father in 1967, and it was there she met and married Steve Newkirk, a race car driver. The couple subsequently moved to Maryland where Ingrid initially began studying for a career as a stockbroker .

Ingrid was, at one time, on the other side of the law, wearing the badge of a sheriff's deputy and a local law enforcement officer in Maryland, both assignments dealing with animal control. She was also, according to a biographical sketch, director of cruelty investigations for the Washington Humane Society, the second oldest humane society in the U.S., and Chief of Animal Disease Control for the Washington's Commission on Public Health. She met Pacheco while she was working at an animal shelter and he was volunteering there.

The organization began in the basement of a Takoma Park, Maryland home with 18 members and staged its first demonstrations in 1980 by picketing a Washington-area poultry slaughterhouse, and the following April, by demonstrating against animal research at the National Institutes of Health.

Now, over 20 years later and with a reported 700,000 members, PETA has a multi-million annual budget for conducting a wide range of activities that include demonstrations and lobbying efforts. Author/editor Daniel T. Oliver at *Alternatives in Philanthropy*, writing for the Capital Research Center in May 1997, stated that PETA's "ultimate goal" is to abolish hunting, fishing and trapping, the use of animals in biomedical research, the raising of farm animals for food and clothing, the use of animals in the production of insulin, and the breeding and owning of pets. Authors Ron Arnold and Alan Gottlieb, writing in their monumental 1994 book *Trashing the Economy* listed PETA as a "job killer" and "economy trasher" for the group's work against the beef industry, medical research and the cosmetics industry.

Listed as a 501 (c) (3) nonprofit organization, PETA has become the best known among animal rights groups, but has steadfastly denied any direct involvement in the kind of terrorist activities for which ALF was proudly taking credit during the period from mid-1991 to Autumn 1992.

Yet, the Michigan criminal court documents leave some nagging questions involving PETA. The sentencing report recounts how, "Investigators learned that immediately before and after the MSU arson, a Federal Express package had been sent to a Bethesda, Maryland address from an individual identifying himself as 'Leonard Robideau'. The first package went to PETA's Newkirk. The second package was intercepted by employees of Federal Express after they discovered that a phony account number had been used to send the package. This second package contained documents that had been stolen from Dr. (Richard) Aulerich during the MSU raid. Also in this package was a videotape of a perpetrator of the MSU crime, disguised in a ski mask. It had been sent from a drop box adjacent to the Ann Arbor hotel where Coronado had rented a room. Analysis of the handwriting on the freight bill for the Federal Express package showed it to be Coronado's."

This passage is found as a footnote at the bottom of a page in the court document: "Significantly, Newkirk had arranged to have the package delivered to her days before the MSU arson occurred."

Investigators would learn later that Maria Blanton, described as "a longtime PETA member," had "agreed to accept the first Federal Express package from Coronado after being asked to do so by Ingrid Newkirk," said the court papers.

If those court documents are correct, why would Newkirk, who has repeatedly professed to have no involvement in the kinds of activities for which ALF has long claimed credit, have arranged days ahead of time to receive a package from Coronado *prior* to an actual event? How would she even have known that package was coming?

This is the same Ingrid Newkirk who, speaking before the National Animal Rights Convention on June 27, 1997 in Arlington, Va., reportedly remarked, "I wish we all would get up and go into the labs and take the animals out or burn them down."

And this is the same PETA whose then-chairman, Pacheco, was quoted by at least two publications (the *New York Times* and the Charleston, WV *Gazette Mail*) that, "Arson, property destruction, burglary and theft are 'acceptable crimes' when used for the animal cause." Pacheco, according to the Michigan court documents, had apparently planned, along with Coronado and others, a 1990 burglary at Tulane University's Primate Research Center, an assertion made on the basis of records and other documents found by federal authorities during a search at Maria Blanton's home.

For criminal investigators, Coronado's case provided mounting evidence that the link between ALF and PETA may be far stronger than the former using the latter as a media go-between after a raid. PETA had also issued press releases and videotapes following ALF raids at the University of Arizona and Texas Tech.

The MSU attack resulted in $125,000 in property damage, but that somewhat glosses over the actual loss, which might arguably have been considerably more in terms of social loss.

Lost in the fire at MSU's Anthony Hall were 32 years of medical research and data, including critical information on the reproduction of endangered species, according to a bulletin from the Americans for Medical Progress Educational Foundation. Likewise, research that had relied on tests on animal DNA – rather than on animals, themselves – was also destroyed.

Timed firebombs were placed in the offices of Dr. Aulerich and his associate, Dr. Karen Chou, who had been conducting the animal DNA tests. When those devices detonated, two students were inside Anthony Hall and it is possible they could have been killed. Fortunately, they escaped unharmed. Aulerich's office, library and research went up in flames.

Law enforcement authorities pressed their investigation because now an arson had come close to endangering human life.

Back To Utah

Months passed following the costly MSU arson. While the investigation into that attack, and the earlier raids in Washington, Oregon and Utah continued, ALF was evidently planning one last raid in the Bite Back operation. This endeavor would take ALF back to the Beehive State, where a raid at Utah State University in Millville was finally carried off the night of Oct. 24, 1992.

Going out with a bang seemed to be what ALF wanted from this operation, and it was costly. Again using a timed incendiary, ALF targeted the university's farm facility where coyotes were being housed and studied as part of a project sponsored by the U.S. Department of Agriculture.

Ironically, this research project was reportedly aimed at studying coyote behavior so that scientists might come up with some methods to protect these predators in the wild.

The coyotes were released and the facility set ablaze, result-ing in over $100,000 in damage.

ALF raiders left their traditional spray-painted initials and other pleasantries on the walls, then issued a press re-lease claiming credit for the attack.

Nine months after the Utah arson and nearly 16 months after the MSU attack, a federal grand jury in Grand Rapids, Mich., handed down a five-count indictment against Coronado. Investigators had tracked his movements, and according to court documents, had placed Coronado in the area of "virtually every ALF attack immediately before or after it occurred." Coronado's problem was that he left a trail of telephone calls that pretty much matched the loca-tions of the attacks.

Linking Coronado to the ALF attacks was the key ele-ment in the investigation, but the link between ALF and PETA seemed to grow stronger, thanks to records seized during the search of Blanton's home. These records, ac-cording to the court documents, "included surveillance logs; code names for Coronado, Pacheco and others; burglary tools; two-way radios; night vision goggles, phony identifi-cation for Coronado and Pacheco; and animal euthanasia drugs."

The investigation also included a search of a storage locker in Talent, Oregon. This locker had been rented by Coronado and inside was a typewriter that forensic exam-iners determined had been used to write a letter outlining planned arsons at two Montana fur farms, and a plea for money to finance the operations. One of those was the Huggans farm that was burglarized in December 1991.

By late 1992, grand juries in several states were busily investigating Operation Bite Back, and they discovered an emerging pattern. Everyone they questioned from the ani-mal rights movement refused to cooperate. Four people including Trimiew and Stout, Coronado's companions in Michigan, plus Jonathan Paul and an author named Rik Scarce, were jailed for contempt even though they had been offered immunity.

By the time the indictment was handed down in 1993, Coronado the terrorist legend had become Coronado the fugitive from justice. He disappeared for the next 16 months while authorities in several states looked for any lead to his whereabouts.

Coronado had assumed yet another identity, that of "Martin Rubio," and he was living on the Pasqua Yaqui reservation near Tucson, Arizona. That was where he was finally arrested by agents with the federal Bureau of Alcohol, Tobacco and Firearms in September 1994.

On March 3, 1995, Coronado pleaded guilty to the MSU arson, and also to the theft of a notebook, kept by a trooper in the doomed 7th Cavalry, from the Little Bighorn National Park in Montana. His fingerprints were found on the glass case that had held the notebook. Coronado burned that irreplaceable journal, and a piece of American history was lost forever.

Paying The Bills

There is a striking parallel between the cases of Roger Troen and Rodney Coronado that goes beyond their both having been convicted for criminal activity in the cause of animal rights.

When their legal bills came due, the first open checkbook belonged to PETA.

Troen's legal defense cost $27,000 and PETA paid the fees. When his $34,900 fine was handed down, PETA paid that, also.

Coronado's legal bill came to $45,200 and once again

PETA provided the cash. In addition, PETA also reportedly gave, or loaned (depending upon which explanation one accepts) another $25,000 to Coronado's father, Ray, who would later have a difficult time recalling exactly what that money was for, or what he did with it.

These are not the only examples of PETA funding being used to support people convicted on charges relating to animal rights offenses, up to and including attempted murder.

In 1988, Fran Stephanie Trutt, a member of Friends of Animals – another extremist group – was convicted of possessing pipe bombs and the attempted murder of Leon Hirsch, president of the U.S. Surgical Company, with a radio-controlled nail bomb. PETA provided $7,500 to her legal defense.

In 2000, PETA contributed $5,000 to the "Josh Harper Support Committee." Harper is an Oregon-based animal rights activist associated with ALF, and he has been in considerable legal trouble over the years, arrested several times and once convicted of assaulting a police officer.

Questioned about this kind of support for animal rights terrorists – and specifically about the Coronado expenditures – in an April 4, 2002 radio interview with Seattle talk station KVI-AM, Newkirk insisted to host Kirby Wilbur, "Most people in the animal rights movement…are against violence."

If that's the official policy at PETA headquarters, the organization has a rather unusual method of demonstrating its disdain. While publicly insisting that PETA is not that closely connected to ALF and other violent animal rights extremists, Newkirk has never been able to fully explain why her organization would contribute the amount of money it has over the years to the defense of individuals from another organization whose actions were destructive and, in the Michigan case and the Trutt case, potentially homicidal?

The argument she has offered occasionally has the rather lofty overtone of supporting the rights of people persecuted in the defense of animals. But it goes deeper than that.

Perhaps Newkirk explained it unintentionally when she told Wilbur, "I think (these tactics) are right...and I think history will show they are right."

Challenged by Wilbur if she condoned and sanctioned such tactics, Newkirk danced around a direct answer and responded disingenuously, "It's like a thunder storm. It's going to happen whether you condone it or not."

Two

DECLARING WAR ON RESEARCH

People For the Ethical Treatment of Animals did not suddenly become publicly linked with the terrorist Animal Liberation Front in mid-1991 during Operation Bite Back.

This was hardly the first incident in which PETA and ALF were connected. Fully two years before the June 1991 arson at Oregon State University, PETA was acting as a sort of news conduit for ALF. This is a curious situation, as it would seem to most rational people that if one was the head of an activist – yet completely above board – organization, one would almost certainly not want to be linked in any way to a radical underground group known widely for its destructive and dangerous clandestine actions against private property and public institutions.

Most assuredly, the very last thing one should want would be to have his organization identified as a public relations front for an outlaw band of arsonists and burglars.

On April 2, 1989, animal rights extremists raided the University of Arizona at Tucson, breaking into two buildings at the campus – the Pharmacy Microbiology Building and the Office of the Division of Animals Resources – to steal a reported 1,000 research animals and set fires that caused $250,000 in damage. ALF claimed the total was closer to $500,000.

The University of Arizona raid was nowhere near as costly as a devastating arson almost exactly two years earlier at the University of California-Davis. On April 16, 1987, the letters "ALF" were left spray-painted on a wall at the John E. Thurman Veterinary Diagnostic Laboratory on the UC Davis campus. The laboratory was heavily damaged, as were 17 vehicles parked nearby.

Ironically, this facility was designed to develop and provide diagnostic information for the control of diseases among animals. Observers might logically look at this single terrorist act and wonder what the perpetrators were thinking, if they were thinking at all.

The fire cost $4.6 million, and it was the third-costliest animal terrorist arson recorded, falling behind the $12 million arson at a Colorado ski resort in 1998, and an attack years later at the University of Washington.

Nobody was ever apprehended or charged in the UC Davis fire.

Of particular interest to those in the medical community, the animals stolen during the University of Arizona raid included laboratory mice that had been infected with a human parasite.

The perpetrators also destroyed research on a deadly bacteria called cryptosporidium, which can be fatal to malnourished children, AIDS patients and anyone else suffering from an immuno-deficiency. Daniel T. Oliver with Alternatives in Philanthropy noted in a 1997 report that an outbreak of cryptosporidium in Milwaukee, Wisconsin had killed 100 people, and there was no known cure.

The following day, PETA issued a press release for ALF, and also provided videotapes apparently made by the perpetrators during the costly burglary.

If there was no connection between PETA and the ALF arsonists, how was it that PETA was so quickly able to get its hands on the videotape of that raid? If PETA does not, and has not, condoned this kind of illegal activity, what was that organization doing by serving as a go-between for ALF and the news media?

Indeed, why did not PETA simply, and very quietly, turn the tapes over to law enforcement, perhaps in the hopes fingerprints or other evidence could be gathered from the cassette or envelope, instead of releasing it to the press?

The same could reasonably be asked months after the destructive University of Arizona raid in April 1989. On the night of Jan. 14, 1990 ALF raiders broke into the University of Pennsylvania office of Dr. Adrian Morrison, a PETA critic who had spoken favorably about the contributions of animal research. Perhaps not surprisingly, PETA almost immediately had copies of the documents stolen from Morrison's office and had written what it called a "preliminary examination" of the material during a demonstration at the university.

Two and a half months after the University of Arizona raid, on July 1, 1989 at Texas Tech University in Lubbock, a vandalism and burglary resulted in about $70,000 in property damage, but overall cost the university an estimated $1 million to repair the damage and replace equipment. While the initial cost paled in comparison to the ALF attack at UC Davis and even the University of Arizona, it eventually became a significant amount of money.

Perhaps more significantly, this raid provided the terrorists with yet another opportunity to speak to the public, using PETA as the intermediary.

What made this attack so costly in human terms was the research that was lost at Texas Tech. The target of this raid was the university's Health Science Center. There, research was being conducted by Dr. John Orem in an attempt to find solutions for various sleep disorders, not the least of which is Sudden Infant Death Syndrome.

The perpetrators left their usual "ALF" trademark spray

painted on the walls, but this time they did not burn anything. Instead, they either stole or released five cats that had been conditioned for the research. They also damaged research equipment, some of it beyond repair.

Following this raid, the laboratory was out of business for 45 days. At the end of that time, the lab had undergone something of a transformation, with new security equipment installed and damaged equipment replaced.

ALF's statement, as released through PETA, said the theft of those laboratory cats was justified. Many would disagree, not the least of which was the *Wall Street Journal*, which editorialized in support of research using animals following the April 1989 attack at Arizona.

The *WSJ* noted that heart research pioneer Dr. Michael De Bakey, and liver transplant authority Dr. Thomas Starzl both "consider the animal rights movement to be one of the greatest threats to continued medical research in the United States."

Terrorism defined?

Two months after the Texas Tech attack, PETA founder Ingrid Newkirk uttered what has since become one of the most famous phrases in the animal rights movement, and a chief target of critics who use the statement as the premier example of faulty thinking.

In the September 1989 issue of *Vogue*, Newkirk insisted that, "Animal liberationists do not separate out the human animal, so there is no rational basis for saying that a human being has special rights. A rat is a pig is a dog is a boy. They're all mammals."

That said – and Newkirk continues to defend the statement today – one might reasonably ask, does she apply the same standard to various levels of animal rights activism?

If "a rat is a pig is a dog is a boy," then why would not an animal rights terrorist from ALF be the same as an animal rights "activist" working for PETA? If there is no special separation of humans from animals, then why should there be any special separation – in the eyes of law enforcement or anyone else – between ALF fanatics who torch buildings, send razor blades to researchers, and commit other criminal acts, and PETA "activists" who claim to be nonviolent while picketing fur markets, clothing stores and other venues?

For example, if one would be justified in defending himself and his property with whatever force necessary against an ALF terrorist, is there any reason why the same individual would not be completely justified in using force immediately against a PETA protester, say near a hunting blind or on a fishing dock? What about the PETA protester who blocks access into and out of a department store, or one who throws blood on someone's fur coat?

Facing an act such as that, would the victim – whether hunter, shopper or property owner – be justified in using physical force against his or her assailant? We will discuss this again in a later chapter.

Consider what happened in 1999 at the UC Davis campus, site of the devastating fire in 1987. Late in 1999, the university adopted a policy of sending some mail addressed to scientists on campus through X-ray machines after booby-trapped letters, containing exposed razor blades, had been received by some primate researchers. All those letters were credited to a fringe organization calling itself the Justice Department, and were mailed to scientists whose names were on a list of 87 animal researchers nationwide that were posted on a website.

In all, seven of those razor blade letters, postmarked Oct. 22 in Las Vegas, were received by researchers at the

University. They were put together with the blades in the envelope flap, according to the university's *Dateline* newsletter of Nov. 5, 1999, so that the individual opening the letter would cut their fingers.

No coincidence here, on Oct. 27, three Harvard scientists also received razor blade letters, on the heels of five others that had been received by researchers at the Harvard laboratory in Southboro. The Justice Department took credit for all of them.

Nobody was hurt, though, because all seven letters sent to UC Davis were detected and turned over to the FBI. One of the letters contained, according to published reports, a note that warned the recipient, "You have been targeted, and you have until autumn of 2000 to release all our primate captives and get out of the vivisection industry. If you do not heed our warning, your violence will be turned back on you."

Newkirk, according to an article on the ConsumerFreedom.com website Nov. 12, 2001, reportedly supported the idea of sending razor blades to researchers, hoping that it "frightens them out of their careers." That quote originally appeared in the Oct. 28 edition of the *Boston Herald*.

This is the same woman who claimed, in a Nov. 5, 2001 commentary appearing on CNSNews.com entitled "PETA Terra-ists" that, "PETA does not condone or commit violent acts, nor do we threaten anybody with violence...Our goal is purely peaceful; we ask people to stop treating animals (and each other) like objects without feelings. The most 'violent' thing we've ever done was to lob a bit of tofu 'cream' pie at a clothing designer who rips the skins from animals' backs. It was more vaudeville than anything else."

Perhaps it was some other person named Ingrid Newkirk who wrote an article entitled "To Market, To Market" in the *Los Angeles Times Magazine* of March 22, 1992 that approved of ALF's outlaw attacks.

Is this where Newkirk should perhaps clarify whether she wants people to do what she says for mass public digestion, or what she suggests to an audience of ostensibly likeminded people?

What constitutes an animal rights terrorist? Using Newkirk's own rationale expressed in her "pig-rat-dog-boy" diatribe, it might be anyone who claims to support animal rights, regardless the degree of devotion.

Does that make Ingrid Newkirk an animal rights terrorist, and PETA a terrorist organization?

ALF's 'P-R Firm?'

One is usually judged by the company one keeps. That has been the advice handed down through countless generations by parents and grandparents, and one might wonder about the possibility of it being accurate when discussing PETA and ALF in terms of domestic terrorism.

When PETA co-founder Alex Pacheco was deposed for testimony bearing on a case called *Berosini v. PETA*, he remarked that PETA is comparable to "a P-R firm for ALF..." Some might consider that an awfully close relationship between what is reportedly the largest animal rights organizations in the world, and a group of loosely-organized violent extremists who burglarize and burn buildings.

The numerous occasions in which PETA has acted as the conduit of public information about an ALF raid or other action have only served to link the organizations inextricably together. Add to that the PETA defense funds contributed to convicted ALF terrorist Rodney Coronado, and there might be a compelling argument that PETA is a front organization for animal terrorists, or that ALF is

PETA's "direct action" arm on a "Mission Impossible" level; if "captured or killed, the secretary will disavow all knowledge of your actions."

That conclusion was reached by author Kathleen Marquardt, with Herbert M. Levine and Mark LaRochelle, in the book *Animal Scam* published by Regnery Gateway in 1994, when she wrote, "PETA and ALF work in a lucrative partnership, profiting from terror."

Marquardt is the founder of Putting People First, an organization that could best be described as the complete opposite of PETA. Established in 1990, Putting People First quickly began racking up a score against PETA and the animal rights movement, emphasizing contradictions in the animal rights movement and message, and hitting them hardest where it evidently hurts the most: In the pocketbook.

Over the years, and more recently in particular, there is ample curiosity about what happens to the millions of dollars that flow to PETA annually. Even before PETA began acting as the spokes-organization for ALF in such cases as the raids in 1989, critics of the organization had been wondering if PETA spent all of its money organizing fur or anti-hunting protests.

That was more than ten years ago, when PETA reported a budget of $11.7 million, according to author Ron Arnold, whose books *Trashing the Economy* and *EcoTerror: The Violent Agenda To Save Nature* have touched on PETA activities. More recently, their budget has climbed to over $15 million. A more precise figure comes from the Better Business Bureau's Wise Giving Alliance which posted, on its Give.org website, PETA's audited financial statement for the fiscal year ending July 31, 2000. According to those figures, PETA pulled in $11,192,814 in contributions and donations, and another $2.43 million in legacies and bequests. Other income brought PETA's total for that year to $16.12 million.

How was that money spent? According to the PETA figures reported by BBB, $14,884,684 went to "program expenses" and there this is how those expenses were broken down:

International grassroots campaigns	$5,222,102
Public outreach and education	4,464,464
Research, investigations and rescue	3,630,346
Supporting organization activities	1,000,000
Cruelty-free merchandise	567,772

It was noted on the BBB website under the heading "Evaluation Conclusions" that, "People for the Ethical Treatment of Animals (PETA) **does not meet** the following CBBB Standard for Charitable Solicitations:

"E3 – Soliciting organizations shall have an independent governing body whose directly and/or indirectly compensated board members constitute no more than one-fifth (20%) of the total voting membership of the board.

"PETA's paid president serves on PETA's three-member board of directors. Therefore, one-third, or 33%, of PETA's board of directors is directly compensated by the organization."

BBB said that PETA meets all of its other standards for charitable organizations, and the one exception may be a somewhat selective criticism. The complaint was about Ingrid Newkirk, who, under the audited figures, took a $29,996 salary for that fiscal year, while Dan Matthews, director of media relations and not a board member, was paid $65,841.

One might reasonably wonder why an organization of PETA's size and stature would ever have allowed itself to be placed in the position of being a conduit of press releases to the media from ALF, especially following incidents such as those in 1989 and 1991.

No Complaints

Why has PETA not complained about ALF using it as a middle-man organization to express its views, take credit for its terrorist acts and pass along veiled threats of more action to come?

Why did PETA not publicly issued an appeal to ALF to stop using it as a go-between?

Other than mouthing generalizations about opposing violence, PETA has never made a serious attempt to distance itself philosophically from ALF.

The reason might just have something to do with the notorious Silver Spring Monkeys case that began unfolding in the spring of 1981, in which it was PETA's Pacheco and Newkirk, not some masked terrorists, who personally pulled off an event that the organization shamelessly used as a fund raising cause, and still does, today, over two decades later.

All that seemed to be missing was a fire and spray-painted walls.

This was the case in which Dr. Edward Taub, a researcher and behavioral scientist working with monkeys in his lab at Silver Spring, Maryland, was indicted on multiple counts of animal cruelty, based almost entirely on evidence produced by Pacheco, and a raid that occurred at the Montgomery County facility on – of all dates – Sept. 11, 1981.

Much has been written and debated about this incident, with all too little attention paid to the fact that Dr. Taub was eventually acquitted of all charges except one, and that one was overturned by the court on appeal.

Taub was working on developing ways to help people

paralyzed by stroke. Today, years after the event that nearly ruined his career, he is hailed for his research.

Taub's biggest mistake in this whole affair was hiring Alex Pacheco as a lab assistant that spring. It just happened that Pacheco lived near Taub's research lab, and he got hired while posing as a student. Over the course of the next four months, Pacheco worked to gain Taub's confidence, even working after hours. That August, while Taub was vacationing, Pacheco photographed one of the 17 experimental monkeys that had been somehow secured improperly to a device that made it appear the animal was being tortured.

During Taub's absences, Pacheco reportedly conducted unofficial visits of the lab for selected activists and persons identified as "academics" to show them the allegedly poor conditions in the facility. On the evening of Sept. 10, Pacheco and Newkirk brought in a veterinarian named Richard Weitzman, who nearly derailed the bogus "investigation" by telling them that, in his opinion, the lab conditions were not that much of a problem. He reportedly also asked why Pacheco and Newkirk had not simply brought their concerns to Taub's attention.

Solving problems was not their goal. Creating controversy and stopping Taub's research – perhaps with the ultimate goal of making money from the effort – seemed to be their motive.

When Taub finally went to trial facing 17 counts, 11 were dismissed by the court and he was acquitted on five others. He appealed the one conviction and that was overturned and dismissed.

Three

PETA'S 'FAVORITE ELF'

Whether Santa Claus has a favorite among his elves, there appears to be one certainty: People for the Ethical Treatment of Animals seems to have a favorite ELF of its own.

Enter the Earth Liberation Front, an organization that is to environmental activism what ALF is to the animal rights movement. They are, according to James Jarboe, Domestic Terrorism Section Chief with the Federal Bureau of Investigation's Counterterrorism Division, one of the more prolific domestic terrorist organizations in the United States.

In testimony before the House Resources Committee Subcommittee on Forests and Forest Health on Feb. 12, 2002, Jarboe noted, "During the past several years, special interest extremism, as characterized by the Animal Liberation Front and the Earth Liberation Front, has emerged as a serious terrorist threat."

That much was made clear in a news release issued by ELF in September 2002, in which the group declared that it would no longer adhere to "a flawed, inconsistent, non-violent ideology."

Instead, in language that cannot be misunderstood, ELF threatened, "...where it is necessary, we will no longer hesitate to pick up the gun to implement justice, and provide the needed protection of our planet that decades of legal battles, pleading protest, and economic sabotage have failed so drastically to achieve."

ELF had issued that communiqué from its "press office" based in Portland, Oregon to claim responsibility for a $700,000 arson at a U.S. Forest Service laboratory in Irvine, Pennsylvania in August 2002. That fire destroyed 70 years of research. In its threatening announcement, ELF promised to strike the facility again, should it be rebuilt.

This constituted the first time that ELF had dropped all pretense of being non-violent, and it drew an immediate response from USFS Law Enforcement Director Bill Wasley. He did not care at all for the threat that ELF terrorists were now considering the use of firearms.

Likewise, Congressman John Peterson, a Pennsylvania Republican, was quoted by the *Washington Times*: "World terrorists are against our economic system, and in reality, these people are, too…I don't know how you rationalize burning down a building where research is being done on how to grow trees better and faster…It's very concerning when you have people willing to blow up buildings and destroy property and to risk life over false issues. They have very twisted minds…"

The August ELF arson and subsequent threat dramatically reinforced Jarboe's February comment to the House subcommittee, "The FBI estimates that the ALF/ELF have committed more than 600 criminal acts in the United States since 1996, resulting in damages in excess of $43 million."

Three weeks after Jarboe's testimony got the undivided attention of the Congressional panel, the *New York Post* headlined a financial connection between ELF and PETA.

True enough, PETA – according to a tax return produced by Richard Berman, executive director of the Center for Consumer Freedom during his testimony before Congress – contributed $1,500 to ELF for what it initially claimed was to "support their program activities

In reality, the $1,500 in question went to help pay for the legal defense of one Craig Rosebraugh, as confirmed by a letter Newkirk sent in response to a CNSNews.com article about the contribution, which appeared March 8, 2002. But this information did not come to the surface without some strenuous prying, because the story kept changing.

When the subject first came up on Feb. 26, 2002, Newkirk told ABC News that she could not recall the contribution.

Newkirk's memory had improved somewhat by March 4, when she told the Associated Press that the check was to pay for "educational materials," though ELF has no history of printing or distributing such materials.

On March 5 – the short span of 24 hours – Newkirk's story had changed, again. According to an account in the Spokane, Washington *Spokesman-Review*, Newkirk told Seattle television station KOMO that the check had been for habitat protection. ELF has no history of legitimate habitat protection projects

Then on March 7, PETA Communications Director Lisa Lange told FOX News that the contribution had been to support a program promoting vegetarianism, just one day before Newkirk's final explanation appeared on CNSNews.com.

One week later, in response to a letter written by Colorado Congressman Scott McInnis (and detailed in the next chapter), PETA attorney Jeffrey Kerr confirmed the money had gone to help in Rosebraugh's defense.

Over the course of four years, from 1997 through fall 2001, Rosebraugh has, according to the Associated Press, acknowledged sending anonymous advisories to the press about ELF attacks during that period.

When he appeared before a congressional hearing chaired by Rep. Scott McInnis (R-CO) under subpoena to testify about ELF activities, Rosebraugh repeatedly invoked the Fifth Amendment right against self-incrimination. He subsequently replied to 57 written questions from the committee, in which, among other things, he expressed support for the notion of property destruction to force social changes.

On the subject of property destruction, only the UC-Davis and Colorado attacks come close to the firebombing that destroyed the University of Washington's Center for Urban Horticulture in Seattle on May 21, 2001. Credit for that $5.3 million blaze was claimed by ALF, but Rosebraugh had this to say about it, according to the Associated Press: "I do not find it disconcerting that ELF firebombed, without physically harming anyone, research into genetic modification of our natural world for profit. Genetic engineering is a threat to life on this planet." So, which was it, ELF or ALF? Perhaps it really doesn't matter.

Amplifying Rosebraugh's remark, in a comment to *Mother Jones.com*, was Elaine Close, an environmental activist based in Portland, Oregon. In an article that appeared on Feb. 8, 2002, Close stated, "This is a battle. The targets are doing something egregious…There's something evil going on, and these groups are trying to stop it."

Yet ELF and ALF claim that they operate under explicit guidelines and their particular definition of "violence." These guidelines insist that "no animal, human or non-human, shall be injured or killed in the course of an action." They further assert that "all necessary precautions are taken to avoid injuring life."

That apparently does not cover plant life, since the U of W inferno destroyed considerable plant life, and it was deliberate.

To underscore the significance of the U of W fire, American Policy Center President Tom DeWeese noted in a March 3, 2002 essay that prior to the terrorist attacks of Sept. 11, 2001 on New York and Washington, D.C., that

Seattle arson was "by far the most destructive act in 2001."

What Is ELF?

One might logically wonder what possible connection there could be between a self-proclaimed non-violent animal rights network and a self-delusional group of environmental criminals that believes its acts of arson and vandalism will somehow change society for the better.

Their goals are somewhat nebulous, other than a professed desire to stop man's destruction of the environment. Or could it be that they have no other motivation than a will to destroy?

ELF has its origins in the early 1990s, when radicals from the extremist environmental group Earth First! (founded by environmental extremist Dave Foreman, who later became a director of the Sierra Club) broke away from the parent organization in Brighton, England. The group first surfaced when it was mentioned in a "joint communiqué" with ALF in 1993, announcing its solidarity with the animal terrorist group.

Where PETA operates openly and insists that it works within the system, frequently going to court or staging daylight protests in front of television cameras, the Earth Liberation Front offers no such pretense. ELF has its own website, which greets visitors with a full-color image of a building going up in flames.

The website claims that since 1997, ELF cells "have carried out dozens of actions resulting in over $30 million in damages." Now, there's an achievement for which ELF's model citizens can be proud. Among its dubious accomplishments are the Jan. 29, 2002 fire at the University of Minnesota's new Microbial and Plant Genomics Research Center. Another act for which ELF claimed gleeful credit is tree spiking in the Nez Perce National Forest in Idaho. ELF also claimed responsibility for burning the Litchfield Wild Horse and Burro facility owned by the Bureau of Land Management (BLM) near Susanville, California in November 2001. These acts barely scratch the surface.

Their activities, both claimed and suspected, go back several years. For example, author Ron Arnold suggested in his book *EcoTerror* (page 51) that bomb blasts on Oct. 31, 1993 in Reno, Nevada at the BLM office, and on March 30, 1995 at a US Forest Service office in Carson City, Nevada might have been the handiwork of ELF terrorists. He based that theory on a notation in the *Earth First Journal* of September-October 1993 (page 34) that the ELF of Germany had called for an "International Earth Night" on Halloween of that year to be part of an "International Action Week" running Oct. 31-Nov. 6. The call to action had the caveat that no group should take credit in order to confuse law enforcement investigations.

Tree spiking – the act of driving large spikes into trees in hopes of damaging or shattering loggers' chainsaws or the band saws in lumber mills, often with disastrous and injurious results to equipment and people – dates back to the early 1980s. One of the most prolific tree spikers may have been Frank Ambrose, who was arrested Jan. 23, 2001 by officers with the Indiana Department of Natural Resources and the Indianapolis Joint Terrorism Task Force. Ambrose had spiked an estimated 150 trees in Indiana state forests, an action for which ELF claimed responsibility.

A month later, Jared McIntyre, Matthew Rammelkamp and George Mashkow pleaded guilty to arson and conspiracy for a series of arsons at construction sites on Long Island, New York. McIntyre reportedly stated that the fires were set in sympathy to ELF's cause.

Perhaps the most disturbing thing about ELF, as with

ALF, is that the organization insists it is not organized at all, but instead is a "non-hierarchical" group, in which "individuals involved control their own activities." Simply put, it is an allegedly disorganized cult of environmental extremists who act independently of one another, or at least in independent cells, with the sole intention of creating havoc.

Who are they? As ELF's own website states, "Because (they) are anonymous, they could be anyone from any community. Parents, teachers, church volunteers, your neighbor, or even your partner could be involved." There is no "official" membership, so there is no accurate measure of how large ELF actually is. Some experts suggest that there may be no more than 100 or 200 hard-core ELF "activists" and far fewer who actually commit any of the illegal acts for which ELF claims responsibility.

As the hunter's axiom goes, "One deer can make a lot of tracks." Likewise, one or two ELF extremists can travel around the country making lots of trouble, leaving the impression that there are more of them, and that they are widespread.

However, the FBI considers ELF a large, active and dangerous domestic terrorist group. ELF has done nothing to refute that image.

ELF claims to be "modeled after the Animal Liberation Front," a statement that clearly paints ALF into a rather tight philosophical corner. ELF lists the following as its guidelines:

> To inflict economic damage on those profiting from the destruction and exploitation of the natural environment.
> To reveal and educate the public on the atrocities committed against the earth and all species that populate it.

> To take all necessary precautions against harm-
> ing any animal, human and non-human.

DeWeese perhaps summed it up best when he noted,
"ALF, ELF and seemingly mainstream advocacy groups have
been given free reign to undertake acts of terrorism or to
seek public acceptance for such acts. That day must now
end. They must be given the same priority as al Qaeda and
other Muslim terrorists. Their objectives may differ, but their
crimes do not."

On the other hand, Elaine Close – described by *Mother
Jones.com* as the "spokesperson for the Earth Liberation
Front's Press Office – suggested that ALF and ELF "are
heroes, as were others in the past who have accepted great
personal risk in the fight against injustice."

Mouthing The Same Mantra

Could one consider Elaine Close and Ingrid Newkirk
sisters in a cause who were separated at birth, or perhaps
remain connected today by a spiritual and philosophical
umbilical cord?

Of the two, Newkirk's career has certainly been more
colorful. Arrested several times, Newkirk has made headlines by splashing herself with fake blood to protest what
she called animal cruelty, and – like Close – has shown no
disdain for the acts of sabotage, vandalism and property
destruction that are the means to justify her ultimate goal
of protecting animals.

There is one other similarity between the two activists:
Neither claims a direct connection, or personal responsibility, for any of the high-profile criminal acts that would result in prison sentences for anyone convicted in those cases.
Indeed, they both tend to demonize those whose activities

they vehemently oppose, deflecting blame from themselves and animal rights terrorists onto the people they would attack.

Here's Close in a Q&A response to MotherJones.com, Feb. 14, 2002: "The word 'terrorism' really has no meaning at this point. Its constant use has become a propaganda tool. Our corporation-run government and media label actions that oppose their policies 'terrorist acts'. They decided who are 'terrorists' according to self-interest, with no rational application of the term..."

Here's Newkirk in a commentary on CNSNews.com, Nov. 5, 2001: "Who is really violent? The people who imprison animals in laboratories and deliberately poison, infect, inject, addict and kill them or those who demand that science be modernized by using more sophisticated, kinder ways to help people? Those who send animals down slaughterhouse ramps with a curse and a sharp kick or those who promote a veggie diet? The people who cage, kill and skin animals for clothes even survivalists don't need any more or those who say 'pleather' beats leather anytime?"

There are strong philosophical bonds between the ecoterrorists of which Arnold wrote in his book, and animal rights activists/terrorists. In many regards, the line gets very fuzzy, if not invisible. It is very telling that on the ALF and ELF websites, the two organizations are repeatedly mentioned in the same breath, and likewise, when Jarboe reported to Congress about domestic terrorism, he all but identified them as a single entity.

ELF claimed credit for the $12 million Vail, Colorado ski facility arson in October 1998. That conflagration destroyed a restaurant, utility building, four ski lifts and a picnic facility.

Two months later, ELF struck again, taking responsibility for a half-million-dollar fire at the US Forest Industries Office in Medford, Oregon.

Like ALF, the "weapon of choice" for ELF is fire, and they have used it in the states of New York, Michigan and Washington in addition to Oregon and Colorado. There is no indication that they have put away the matches, and with a heightened attention to terrorism both foreign and domestic in the months since the Sept. 11 attacks, it is possible that ALF and ELF extremists have simply gone to ground for a while, until they believe it is safer for them to strike again without getting caught.

In the meantime, there are far less violent demonstrations being conducted by PETA, such as the May 10, 2002 appearance by PETA's Lisa Franzetta in Seattle, dressed in a "pleather" (imitation leather) dominatrix outfit, complete with whip, trying to call public attention to alternatives to leather.

Franzetta is no stranger to such publicity stunts. The very shapely and attractive Ms. Franzetta is perhaps most famous for her appearance in central Hong Kong on Feb. 28, 2002, with fellow activist Kristie Phelds. Much to the delight of a lunchtime crowd, Franzetta and Phelds paraded with signs protesting the use of fur and leather, and very little else.

Sometimes called PETA's "Tiger Lady," (an identity she apparently shares with Cynthia Lieberman, who appeared in a thong, pasties and painted-on tiger stripes on May 29, 2001 in a Shreveport, Louisiana protest against alleged circus animal abuse) Franzetta seems to like taking off her clothes in support of animal rights. She's done it all over the map.

PETA also held the "Compassion Conference" in Seattle in April 2002, with Newkirk in attendance, hosting a vegetarian lunch.

'A Matter Of Time'

Colorado Congressman McInnis chaired the Congressional inquiry into domestic terrorism before his House Resources Committee Subcommittee on Forests and Forest Health in February 2002. This was the event – the Oversight Hearing on Eco-Terrorism and Lawlessness on the National Forests – that found Rosebraugh invoking the Fifth Amendment over 50 times.

At the time, Rep. George Nethercutt (R-WA), was so bemused that he asked Rosebraugh if he were in any way related to former Enron executive Kenneth Lay, who had also testified that day, and also repeatedly invoked the Fifth Amendment during Congressional testimony on the Enron scandal.

Mindful of the kind of destruction that can, and has, been caused by animal rights and environmental terrorists, McInnis sent a letter to Newkirk, asking seven specific questions of the PETA founder, including the identity of the individual from ELF who endorsed the now-infamous $1,500 check PETA sent to ELF for the Craig Rosebraugh legal defense.

Theoretically, authorities might be able to question that individual to learn the identities of other ELF terrorists. However, they may not have far to look, because the signature on that check reportedly was Rosebraugh's.

The ELF contribution is important on several levels, not the least of which would be to completely undermine any credibility that PETA might retain with Capitol Hill, by now a rather tenuous proposition. Any such credibility may have already been destroyed by the repeatedly changing explanations about the money that had been provided between Feb. 26 and March 14.

PETA attorney Kerr – who indicated that it was

Rosebraugh's signature on the PETA check – wrote in his letter of response to Rep. McInnis that, "PETA does not provide financial or any other assistance to any person or group for the purpose of so-called terrorist activities. Any suggestion to the contrary is simply wrong, defamatory, and the product of lobbyists, public relations consultants and other paid spokespeople for animal-exploitive industries."

If that is true, why did PETA contribute that $1,500 to Rosebraugh's defense effort, then offer several different explanations for it? Even if the money hadn't gone to Rosebraugh, it was still ostensibly earmarked to support ELF's "program activities." The only "programs" for which ELF has ever taken credit are arsons and other property destruction.

Perhaps too much attention has been given to that donation to Rosebraugh, blowing it out of perspective. Taken in context, it is a pittance compared to the other contributions which Kerr may feel obliged to justify, including that $45,200 to the defense of ALF terrorist Rodney A. Coronado, and never pushed for repayment of the $25,000 "loan" to his father.

And Mr. Kerr, could you explain why did PETA pay the legal expenses and fine – a total of $61,900 – for activist Roger Troen following his conviction in the Oregon State University case?

What was PETA thinking when it contributed that $5,000 to the "Josh Harper Support Committee?"

For what reason did PETA feel compelled in 1988 to donate that $7,500 to Fran Stephanie Trutt's legal defense?

And finally, Kerr just might be able to account for what David Wilson, the Utah-based animal rights activist who was identified as the "national spokesperson" for ALF did with the $2,000 PETA gave him in 1999.

Compared to all of these so-called "grants", the donation to Rosebraugh is significant only in that it continues PETA's highly questionable pattern of financial support for animal rights and environmental terrorists.

One could reasonably ask the attorney: What might the organization expect to receive in return for all of this financial support? What *has* it received, if anything?

These are not questions designed to defame PETA, although – in the minds of some people, at least – the answers might. The author wants to make that perfectly clear, because Kerr is pretty quick to accuse people of defamation. He accused Congressman McInnis of working with corporate enemies of PETA in an attempt to defame the organization.

In response, McInnis rather forcefully observed that the nature of the people into whose activities his committee was delving are deserving of the attention: "These are hardened criminals. They are dangerous, they are well-funded, they are savvy, sophisticated and stealthy, and if their violence continues to escalate, it is only a matter of time before their parade of terror results in a lost human life."

Four

TRACKING THE MONEY
(There's Lots Of It!)

Wa*shington Post* reporter Bob Woodward developed a source during his investigation of the Watergate break-in whom he called "Deep Throat." This source was allegedly a Nixon White House insider; someone who knew enough to provide leads to Woodward so he and fellow reporter Carl Bernstein could unravel the cover-up that brought down a president and tested the strength of our constitutional government.

Early in that investigation, Deep Throat – whose identity remains a secret 30 years later – gave Woodward some advice that holds true even today, on other stories: Follow the money.

When one begins looking at the animal rights movement, and its flagship organization, People for the Ethical Treatment of Animals, one quickly discovers that there is a lot of money to be followed. It takes you to some rather interesting places, and introduces you to some interesting people.

Ingrid Newkirk, co-founder of PETA, is also a director of the Foundation to Support Animal Protection (FSAP).

Another director of that foundation is Dr. Neal Barnard, the founder of Physicians Committee for Responsible Medicine (PCRM). In September 1999, Bernard and PCRM issued a press release in which he declared, "Meat consumption is just as dangerous to public health as tobacco use." PCRM reported an income of $2,919,047 for the 2000 fiscal year, and it spent $2,915,847, according to data published by the Center for Consumer Freedom (CCF).

According to William T. Jarvis, editor of the National Council Against Health Fraud's (NCAHF) newsletter, Dr. Barnard is a "medical adviser" to PETA, and he suggested that Barnard's group "may be substantially funded" by PETA. The financial data appears to support that assertion.

Wrote Jarvis: "In NCAHF's view, PCRM is a propaganda machine whose press conferences are charades for disguising its ideology as news events."

According to CCF, "the group's member physicians represent less than 0.5% of America's doctors."

Dr. Barnard is a well-known promoter of vegan diets, and a much-published author on the subject. He also campaigns against the use of animals in medical research.

A bit of research using CCF data uncovered the following: between 1988 and 1999, PETA contributed $185,026 directly to PCRM. More importantly, though, in 1999-2000, the Foundation to Support Animal Protection – that non-profit for which Newkirk and Barnard both serve as directors – funneled $592,524 to PCRM. That was significant enough for the CCF to assert, in a press release, that "PETA has used their closely controlled Foundation to Support Animal Protection to launder over $500,000 in contributions to (PCRM), an organization whose president collaborates with a violent animal rights group known as Stop Huntington Animal Cruelty (SHAC)."

Barnard co-signed a letter with SHAC's Kevin Jonas (Kjonass) – frequently identified as "a former ALF spokesman" – urging customers of the Huntingdon Life Sciences, a British-based research facility, to stop doing business with

Huntingdon. That facility, and its employees, have been the target of sometimes violent animal rights actions.

On the evening of Thursday, Feb. 22, 2001, HLS Managing Director Brian Cass was attacked and beaten outside his home by three masked and hooded men using baseball bats or pickaxe handles, depending upon which account one accepts. On Aug. 16 of that year, one of the three, David Blenkinsop, was convicted in the attack and sentenced to three years in prison. The other two attackers were still on the loose.

When Blenkinsop was arrested, he was at an animal sanctuary operated by British television script writer Carla Lane

Other donors sympathetic to the animal rights philosophy or a radical environmental agenda also contribute to PCRM.

There was $30,000 from the Helen Brach Foundation, 1998-2000. This foundation also gave $15,000 in 1998-99 to United Poultry Concerns, which opposes eating chicken, turkey and other poultry, and eggs. The foundation is named for Helen Voorhees Brach, an heiress to the E.J. Brach & Sons Candy Company and widow of the late Frank Brach. The Brach Foundation also gave $10,000 to PETA in 1995.

Newkirk serves on the advisory board for United Poultry Concerns.

In 2000, the Glaser Family Foundation contributed $30,000 to PCRM. The Glaser foundation was created by Seattle computer software giant Ron Glaser, CEO of RealNetworks, Inc. This foundation lists "animal advocacy" as one of its missions on its website. Between 1999 and 2001, the Glaser Foundation also donated $179,488 to PETA.

The Geraldine R. Dodge Foundation awarded a $20,000 welfare of animals grant to PCRM in 2001 for its campaign "to end the use of live animals in medical education." This foundation also gave $40,000 to Utah State University for "a research project that will explore the psychological motivation of animal abusers who batter women." The Dodge Foundation also gave $105,000 to the avowed anti-hunting organization, Humane Society of the United States to support its "Leadership Development for Animal Care and Control Professionals" project.

Another $10,000 for PCRM came from the Park Foundation in 2000. This foundation also is a heavy supporter of PETA, contributing $200,000 from 1997-1999. The Park Foundation also gave $10,000 to United Poultry Concerns in 1998.

Perhaps the most notable contribution found by the author was not the most generous, but it provided a significant philosophical link. That was the $8,000 donation from the Benjamin J. Rosenthal Foundation during the 1997-2000 period. This foundation was created by the heirs of Rosenthal, who founded the Chicago Mail Order House.

The Rosenthal Foundation also gave $8,000 to PETA during the same period, but what is most interesting is that one of Rosenthal's heirs is Elaine Broadhead, a large contributor to the Ruckus Society and Rainforest Action Network. The foundation gave $11,000 to Ruckus during the same period.

The Ruckus Society was founded by Earth First! cofounder Mike Roselle, and it is given much credit for the WTO riots in Seattle in November-December 1999. According to CCF's Richard Berman, Ruckus "trains young activists in the techniques of 'monkey wrenching' which, when applied, result in property crimes of enormous financial cost."

More Support & Connections

Don't put away that calculator, there's more! Other major contributions to both PETA and PCRM come from a variety of tax-free sources.

For example, the Judi & Howard Strauss Foundation gave PETA $18,500 in 1998-2000, and $10,000 to PCRM in 1998.

The Komie Foundation gave a whopping $40,000 to PETA in 1998-99 and another $9,000 to PCRM in 1997-99. This same foundation donated $11,200 to United Poultry Concerns in 1998-99 and $6,000 to the Farm Animal Reform Movement (FARM) in 1997-99.

PETA gets singled out by other foundations, and there is no indication whether that money remains with PETA or becomes part of the subsequent support PETA provides to PCRM.

The Philanthropic Collaborative – which donated $111,000 to the Natural Resources Defense Council in 1997-99 – gave PETA $25,600 during that same time period.

PETA received $23,400 in 1998-2000 from the Pond Foundation, which also gave $108,000 to the Natural Resources Defense Council in 1998-99, $48,600 to Greenpeace in 2000 and $37,800 to the Organic Consumers Association in 1998-2000.

The San Francisco Foundation gave PETA $7,000 in 2000, while the Lynn R. and Carl E. Prickett Fund gave PETA $5,000 in 1999.

Perhaps not surprising, Newkirk and Bernard also serve as advisory board members to another radical vegetarian organization, EarthSave International (ESI). This vegan group has received financial support from the Mary Reynolds Babcock Foundation ($30,000 in 1992), the Roy A. Hunt Foundation ($12,000 in 1998-99), the Energy Foundation ($10,000 in 1992) and the Richard & Rhoda Goldman Fund ($10,000 in 1993).

ESI has less to do with saving the planet then it does with promoting vegetarianism. Founded by John Robbins as "a global movement of people from all walks of life who are taking concrete steps to promote healthy and life-sustaining food choices" (according to ESI's website), it gets closest to the environmental movement by claiming that raising animals for food is destructive to the ecology.

On the ESI Advisory Board are PCRM founder Dr. Neal Barnard and PCRM Advisory Board members T. Colin Campbell, Lawrence Kushi, John McDougall, Dean Ornish and Andrew Weil.

Robbins is the heir to the Baskin-Robbins ice cream fortune and sits on the national council of the Farm Animal Reform Movement. In 2000-2001, PETA contributed $7,000 to FARM, according to the Consumer Freedom Foundation.

In addition to the contribution from the Komie Foundation noted earlier, other FARM contributors include the Humane Society of the United States, which contributed $2,500 in 1997, the Fund for Animals with a $2,000 donation in 2000, and the American Anti-Vivisection Society also donated $1,000 in 2000.

And look who is named, among others, to the FARM National Council: ESI President Howard Lyman, and ESI Advisory Board Members Casey Kasem, Jeremy Rifkin and Frances Moore Lappe.

Indeed, a look at the "Who's Who" in the animal rights community reveals that a lot of the same names continue turning up on advisory boards and councils as one examines the available rosters.

This would not be significant but for something author Ron Arnold said during an interview about his years of dealing with PETA.

"The correct name for that outfit should be 'Three People for the Ethical Treatment of Animals,' because that's all there is on the board," Arnold observed. "They're not democratically elected, they are self-perpetuating."

That said, it appears that there may be far fewer animal rights activists, including the violent extremists, than their activities might lead one to believe. Every social movement will attract a certain number of people, including handfuls of "fringe types" who are drawn to activism not so much because they believe in a cause, but for any number of other reasons, not the least of which is that they simply want to cause trouble.

Others are drawn to demonstrations or conferences perhaps by curiosity or a genuine concern for animals, but they are not the hardcore extremists.

The overwhelming majority of these people never receive a penny for their endeavors. That Rodney Coronado received the $45,200 from PETA to help with his legal defense (and his father got the $25,000 "loan," which was apparently never repaid, according to the Consumer Freedom Foundation) is probably the most significant exception, followed by the $27,000 that PETA provided in legal fees, and the $34,900 payment of fine for ALF "associate" Roger Troen, the convicted University of Oregon raider.

It would be incorrect to call such donations "pay" or even compare the two, as there is no evidence that Coronado, Troen and others for whom PETA has provided financial support in their legal dilemmas are, or ever were, employees of PETA, nor is there any indication that they have ever been under any contractual agreement with the organization.

However, there are nagging questions about such contributions. In a sworn deposition made by Gary Thorud, (identified by author Ron Arnold as a "PETA defector,") during the case of *Berosini v. PETA*, Thorud stated under oath about the payments made on behalf of Roger Troen, "We were illegally funding this individual with money solicited for other causes, and Ingrid [Newkirk] was using that money, bragging to the staff that she had spent $25,000 in the case."

For the record, PETA sued Thorud for making that, and other anti-PETA statements.

For the most part, at least for the "typical" terrorists, the only reward may be the thrill of watching a building burn, and inflicting a financial loss on the victims.

The Seven Questions

On March 4, 2002, Rep. Scott McInnis (R-CO), serving as chair of the House Resources Committee Subcommittee on Forests and Forest Health – which was holding the Oversight Hearing on Eco-Terrorism and Lawlessness on the National Forests reported in Chapter Three – sent the letter to PETA's Newkirk that was previously mentioned.

This was no ordinary letter, and it has become something of a point of discussion on the Internet. Noting that, "…evidence was submitted by one of the Subcommittee's witnesses showing that the People for the Ethical Treatment of Animals contributed to the Earth Liberation Front…" McInnis asked seven specific questions of Newkirk.

The Colorado congressman – no doubt recalling the devastating Vail fire – also noted in his letter, "As a nonprofit organization with tax-exempt privileges and the incumbent public policy obligations that status entails, PETA has a responsibility to explain the full extent of its involvement with and contributions to environmental terror groups like ELF and ALF."

And then came the questions:

> Since 1993, how much and on how many occasions has PETA made financial contributions to either the Earth Liberation Front and/or its press office, the Animal Liberation Front and/or its press office, and suspected or convicted persons associated with ELF and ALF?
>
> Does PETA have any internal policies or guidelines either encouraging or discouraging financial support of unlawful groups like ELF and ALF? If so, what are they?
>
> Under what rational (sic) did PETA make a contribution(s) to ELF?
>
> What steps did PETA take to ensure that these funds would not be used for unlawful purposes? Whose signature appeared on the returned check that PETA gave ELF?
>
> Does PETA condone the violent activities of organizations like ELF? Should PETA's contribution to ELF be seen as an endorsement?
>
> Does PETA have any intention of contributing to ELF, ALF or other similarly motivated groups in the future?

According to a congressional staffer, PETA attorney Jeffrey Kerr's March 14 response to the letter was marked "confidential" and is being treated as such by the McInnis committee. Despite that, excerpts of the letter have appeared in various publications. That staffer told the author that Kerr responded to five specific items in his letter.

If PETA has nothing to hide, why would its attorney mark his response to McInnis "confidential?"

If Ingrid Newkirk has nothing to hide, why would the response to McInnis' letter to her be written by a PETA attorney?

It was Kerr who suggested that it was Rosebraugh's signature on the PETA check. Nobody has so far refuted or "corrected" that conclusion.

The ELF contribution was made, as Kirk acknowledged after PETA had claimed otherwise, to help Rosebraugh. And even if it had not been, if the contribution had been assigned specifically to support ELF "program activities" as was initially asserted, how disingenuous is that? Aren't ELF's typical "program activities" largely considered criminal acts?

One might conclude on the basis of history alone that PETA has made no effort to ensure that funds it contributed to ELF or other groups would not be used to support some criminal activity.

As to whether PETA condones illegal and/or violent activities by ALF, ELF and other such groups, perhaps one need only read Newkirk's observation about nonviolent tactics versus violent ones.

"Our nonviolent tactics are not as effective," she's explained. "We ask nicely for years and get nothing. Someone makes a threat and it works."

Five

SPORTSMEN IN THE CROSSHAIRS

Research and fur farming make animal rights extremists angry. Hunting, and lately fishing, seems to make them crazy.

To demonstrate the limits of that irrationality, one need only look to the PETA website and check a file with "Frequently Asked Questions" about hunting and examine their answers. You would find this interesting exchange:

Q. Isn't hunting okay as long as I eat what I kill?"

A. Did the fact that Jeffrey Dahmer ate his victims justify his crimes? What is done with a corpse after its murder doesn't lessen the victim's suffering."

PETA's Bruce Friedrich, identified as the organization's Vegan Campaign coordinator, has suggested that hunters are comparable to "Nazi doctors and slave traders." This is the same man who was arrested in July 2001 at London's Buckingham Palace for streaking naked toward President George W. Bush as he arrived on a state visit, the only thing on his body being the words "go vegan." Friedrich was arrested for that escapade, but the charge of disorderly behavior was later dropped.

One might consider Friedrich a "one-man international incident." Just six months earlier, on Jan. 18, Friedrich — using a fake press credential — gained access to a lunch of the U.S. Conference of Mayors in Washington, D.C. There, in front of horrified elected officials, Friedrich (posing as a reporter) asked London, England Mayor Ken Livingstone about a plan to chase pigeons out of Trafalgar Square. Friedrich then told Livingstone that the plan was "all wet" before throwing a glass of water in the visiting mayor's face. The PETA activist was grabbed by security personnel and quickly removed from the room.

To reduce wildlife populations, particularly among game species such as deer or elk, PETA recommends taking steps to reduce the fertility of the animals. This has been tried in some places with varying degrees of failure (not success).

An alternative would be to hire sharpshooters to kill animals if necessary, a rather expensive proposition that actually gets closer to what the animal rights extremists consider "murder" than the act of killing an animal during a hunt. Yet in some cases, there has been greater acceptance for the use of government gunmen to cull wildlife populations rather than allow them to be killed by hunters; the aversion apparently being less against killing than the horrid thought that some outdoorsman or woman may find recreational enjoyment in the stalk, and culinary delight later at the table.

For the benefit of those who may be squeamish about the "K"-word, for the remainder of this chapter let us be entirely honest. Wheat and corn are harvested. Game animals are killed. There are many in the hunting community who have tried over the years to speak about hunting and taking game in rather lofty terms – and present that image to the non-hunting public – apparently hoping to make the practices more acceptable to those who don't hunt, but the animals we shoot are no less deceased.

As an award-winning outdoor writer and editor, I have never felt the necessity to sanitize what I do, or apologize for it. The deer in my freezer is just as dead as is the stalk in my vegetable garden from whence came the ear of corn, after it has been broken off and mulched back into the soil or tossed in the compost bin.

A question which animal rights extremists who promote vegetarianism have never adequately answered: If a "rat is a pig is a dog is a boy," then would that not make "a human, an animal an insect a vegetable?" Do vegetables, as living things, have the same rights as a lab rat? If a hunter or angler really wants to start an argument with an animal rights zealot, those are at least two of the questions that might be asked.

Most importantly of all, did the game animal go quickly and humanely, or did it suffer a painful, lingering death?

By its own admission, PETA has no problem with the latter, noting on its website, "Starvation and disease are unfortunate, but they are nature's way of ensuring that the strong survive. Natural predators help keep prey species strong by killing only the sick and weak."

It's okay if animals die of starvation or disease, and it is just fine if an animal has its throat ripped open, and is still alive while a pack of hungry predators start eating, but it is not acceptable for an animal to die suddenly, then be eaten by humans.

Perhaps that explains Newkirk's statement in the June 1990 *Reader's Digest*: "Humans have grown like a cancer. We're the biggest blight on the face of the earth."

Or why, way back in 1983, she was quoted by the *Washington Post* stating, "I don't have any reverence for life, only for the entities themselves."

Also, it remains pretty much a myth that only the weak animals die. A healthy mountain lion can, for example, pull down two healthy deer a week to sustain itself.

However, in California on two different occasions, mountain lions considered past their prime or otherwise unable to hunt wild animals are known to have killed and partly eaten joggers. Mountain lion hunting was banned in

California some years ago, thanks in large part to political and social pressure brought by animal rights extremists, and the cougar population has exploded.

PETA and its followers speak of hunters as a powerful lobby, much the same way that gun control proponents describe and visualize firearms rights organizations such as the National Rifle Association and Citizens Committee for the Right to Keep and Bear Arms. PETA complains that "Powerful hunting lobbies in 35 states have persuaded lawmakers to enact 'hunter harassment' laws that make it illegal for nonhunters to interfere in behalf of animals targeted by hunters..." PETA says the laws are being challenged on constitutional grounds.

While noting that a Connecticut harassment law was struck down, there is nary a mention that harassment laws in New Jersey, Montana, Missouri and Illinois have been upheld. The case in Montana is particularly educational, not only for its example about the lengths to which a hunt protester might go, but also about how the courts should *not* deal with such individuals. The author covered that story while serving as managing editor of the now-defunct *Hunter Education Instructor*, a newspaper that served as an official journal for the International Hunter Education Association.

On March 13, 1990, an anti-hunter named John Lilburn deliberately stepped in front of a rifle being aimed by hunter Hal Slemmer during a special bison hunt outside Yellowstone National Park in Montana. This hunt was designed to control the bison herd, and it also provided the participating hunters with a good supply of meat.

Lilburn, then 41 years old, placed himself in front of Slemmer's muzzle, endangering himself and violating Montana's statute against hunter harassment in the process. Lilburn was arrested and prosecuted, all the while maintaining that it was his right under the First Amendment to interfere with Slemmer's hunt.

Tried and convicted in 1992, Lilburn appealed and an appellate judge tossed out the conviction on the grounds that the Montana statute was unconstitutional. However, the state appealed that ruling to the Montana Supreme Court, and the appeals court was reversed when the state high court said the harassment statute *was* constitutional. Lilburn was ordered to stand trial again. On March 28, 1995, he was convicted.

What then happened is an example of how *not* to treat an animal rights extremist who puts himself, and others, at dangerous peril. Lilburn was given a 30-day suspended sentence and ordered to perform 40-hours of community service, and fined a pitiful $15 to cover court administrative costs.

It is cases like the Lilburn offense that have led to passage of hunter harassment laws in nearly every state, and the federal Recreational Hunting Safety and Preservation Act of 1994. This little-known legislation was passed as part of the 1994 Crime Bill created during the Clinton Administration. It provides for civil penalties against people who intentionally interfere with a lawful hunt on federal land.

Who Talks, Who Walks

It is said among outdoorsmen that there are those who "talk the talk" and those who "walk the walk."

These same outdoorsmen will tell you in somewhat rough language that "Money talks and bullshit walks."

There is a bit of truth in both adages, and it appears from statistics and history that hunters and fishermen are not simply talking the talk about "animal welfare" in terms of preserving, protecting and enhancing wildlife habitat, they also walk the walk.

In 1937, sportsmen supported passage of the Pittman-Robertson Act, which is the Federal Aid in Wildlife Restoration program. Under this program, federal excise taxes charged on the sale of firearms, ammunition and other outdoor equipment is apportioned back to the state fish and wildlife agencies for use in wildlife management and habitat enhancement.

Then, in 1950, using the same excise tax approach, fishermen supported passage of the Dingell-Johnson Act, otherwise known as the Federal Aid in Sportfish Restoration program.

Together, these programs have raised over $5.2 billion for fish and wildlife programs.

PETA and other animal rights organizations have not spent a penny to fund such programs, which not only enhance natural habitat for game animals, but concurrently benefit so-called "non-game" species which are not hunted, but which live and usually thrive in the same habitat.

For example, waterfowl habitat is also home to shorebirds, fur-bearers and fish species. Vast expanses of public and private land which shelter and feed deer and elk herds are also home to countless varieties of bird life and smaller animals. The same environments are used by bears, foxes, coyotes, rabbits and other mammals.

The U.S. Fish & Wildlife Service – a branch of the Department of Interior – manages the National Wildlife Refuge System. These refuges were created largely under pressure by hunters and anglers, with a visionary boost from the late President Theodore Roosevelt, himself a renowned big game hunter, who wanted to preserve, for all time, healthy environments for fish and wildlife. President Roosevelt created the first National Wildlife Refuge in 1903 on a small island off the east coast of Florida to protect pelicans and other species from market hunters. Today, there are some 93 million acres of public land set aside in 531 refuges across the United States.

Animal rights activists despise the very existence of these refuges, claiming that they were created only to grow more animals for hunters to kill, and more fish for anglers to catch. Perhaps so, but today's fish and wildlife populations are on the rebound, and in some cases there have been genuine success stories for which only hunters could claim credit.

The state of wild turkeys in this country was pretty poor only a quarter-century ago. In 1973, according to the National Wild Turkey Federation (NWTF), there were only 1.3 million wild turkeys remaining in the nation. Today, thanks to enhancement efforts that have included turkey transplants to suitable habitat across the country, the population has risen to 5.6 million birds.

The Rocky Mountain Elk Foundation (RMEF), created in 1984, has grown to 132,000 members nationwide, and they have raised tens of millions of dollars to purchase and preserve critical elk habitat. Today, the elk population across the United States hovers at an estimated one million animals. Populations have returned to states where elk had not been seen for years, including Pennsylvania and Arkansas. Many people attend RMEF fund raising events even though they have never seen an elk in the wilds, and realize they quite possibly never will.

In addition to NWTF and RMEF, other hunter-based organizations have long histories of raising funds for the purchase and protection of habitat that benefits not only game species, but other wildlife. Perhaps most famous of all is Ducks Unlimited, which dates back to 1937 and today has more than 60,000 supporters. Over the years this organization has raised millions of dollars for waterfowl habitat in both the United States and Canada.

Founded in 1977, the Foundation for North American Wild Sheep (FNAWS) now boasts a dozen chapters in the United States and Canada, and even more affiliate organizations. Its purpose is to protect and expand populations of wild sheep. Since its creation, FNAWS has raised a reported $18 million to support a variety of projects.

Pheasants Forever, founded in 1982, boasts some 90,000 members and 550 chapters nationwide. They have developed more than a million acres of pheasant habitat over the past two decades and reportedly undertake 25,000 projects each year.

Also founded in 1982, Whitetails Unlimited works for the improvement of whitetail deer herds and enhancement of their habitat.

Quail Unlimited, established in 1981, has 520 chapters nationwide. In 2001 alone, the organization spent over $2.35 million on habitat projects, planting over 1.8 million pounds of seed, 10,000 acres of warm season grasses and distributed more than 2.1 million pounds of wildlife seed for food plots. They also supported 38 research projects, and sponsored over 700 landowner seminars and educational activities.

The Mule Deer Foundation has chapters in 15 western states, raising money for habitat projects and research efforts.

The Ruffed Grouse Society dates back to October 1961 in Virginia. It now has 130 chapters in the United States and Canada, representing some 23,000 members. They raise over $1 million in contributions annually for research, education and habitat enhancement for a bird that, in some areas, is common as dirt and considered dumb as a post by local outdoorsmen. As with all other game species, the grouse shares this habitat with other wildlife, which benefits collaterally from all the attention.

Trout Unlimited is a nationwide fisherman's association founded over 40 years ago, and it also has raised millions of dollars for fish habitat and projects aimed at improving water conditions, and enhancing fish populations.

The Bass Anglers Sportsmen's Society does far more than just operate bass fishing tournaments around the country. They have an active conservation effort aimed at improving water quality and fish habitat, and have supported research on various fish projects, all benefiting more species than bass.

All of these private organizations operate pretty much along the same basic guideline, raising money through member contributions and a series of regional annual banquets featuring auctions that bring in tens of thousands of dollars per event. BASS and Trout Unlimited also raise money through tournaments, and industry support.

There is no historical evidence that PETA or other extremist animal rights organizations have contributed money to purchase habitat for elk, deer, or any other wildlife. As noted earlier, they would count on predators and maybe even disease to reduce wildlife populations, as an alternative to hunting. They encourage landowners to post their property with "No Hunting" signs, and to form anti-hunting organizations or protest hunting.

To exemplify just how bizarre PETA's reasoning can be on the subject, on Nov. 16, 2001, while driving back to PETA headquarters at about 1 a.m. following an anti-hunting "campaigning tour," a Honda Civic belonging to PETA collided with a deer while southbound on the New Jersey Turnpike near Woolwich Township.

PETA staffers Dan Shannon and Jay Kelly were aboard. The car sustained about $6,000 in damages, and about three months later, on Feb. 14, 2002, PETA attorney Matthew

Penzer notified New Jersey Division of Fish & Wildlife Director Bob McDowell that Shannon and Kelly were reserving the right to sue the agency for injuries, and damage to the vehicle.

In a letter to McDowell, Penzer wrote, "PETA, Mr. Shannon and Mr. Kelly believe that this collision, which occurred near the start of New Jersey's hunting season, was caused by the state's Department of Environmental Protection Fish and Wildlife Division and the Fish and Game Council as a result of their deer management program, which includes, in certain circumstances, an affirmative effort to increase deer populations. Despite the known dangers an increased deer population poses to motorists in the state, the Division and Council actively assist in increasing the deer population for the purpose of enhancing hunting opportunities and license revenues..."

In a related press release, PETA's Penzer claimed that the deer was "...fleeing hunters' guns."

Not at 1 a.m. in the morning. But that small fact seems to have eluded PETA, which was after publicity and money. The accident was the fault of hunters and game managers, and could not have been PETA's fault, or more appropriately, no one's fault. Naturally, nobody at PETA wept much for the deer, but it must have been some small consolation that the animal did not die from a hunter's bullet.

While volunteer sportsmen's organizations in virtually ever state donate their time and energies to habitat improvement projects, ranging from enhancing fish ponds to improving timber and range lands that can support big game, PETA encourages people to "play loud radios and spread deer repellent or human hair (from barber shops) near hunting areas." In other words, commit acts of sabotage to interfere with hunters.

Admittedly, the people who do the enhancement

projects like to hunt and fish, and eat the fish and game they take home. It is a part of their culture and heritage, to which they are devoted. The fact that they may only kill fish and game during certain times of the year does not reduce their dedication to the protection of the environment for all species, only sharpens it.

Bashing Boy Scouts

For some years, anglers were not too concerned about the activities of such organizations as PETA and the radicals it inspired. After all, they were busy routing hunters, and leaving fishermen pretty much alone.

That was before PETA declared that "Fishing Hurts." Following on the heels of that monumental "discovery," PETA launched a campaign that could have hardly endeared the organization to middle America, if that was PETA's intent.

The animal rights group declared war on the Boy Scouts.

For many years, one of the merit badges for which a Boy Scout could qualify is for fishing. In the eyes of PETA, it must have been tantamount to teaching young men to torture children, or was this just another opportunity for PETA to seek publicity?

PETA called fishing "hunting in the water." It declared that "Fishing is also inconsistent with the Boy Scout law, which states, 'A Scout understands there is strength in being gentle. He treats others as he wants to be treated. He does not hurt or kill harmless things without reason.' Clearly, there is no reason to inflict the pain and suffering that fish endure at the hands of anglers."

PETA's campaign claimed that "cruelty to animals is a warning sign often seen in people who eventually direct violence toward humans."

One can only surmise how the Boy Scouts felt about hearing that. Possibly, they felt the same when anti-gun zealots criticized the Scout's merit badge program for rifle marksmanship.

PETA did not stop at half-measures in its campaign. It encouraged people to send letters to Milton H. Ward, president of the Boy Scouts, demanding that the merit badges for fishing and "Fish and Wildlife Management" be replaced with a merit badge for "Waterway Cleanup." It also encouraged creating merit badges for "other humane outdoor activities" including hiking and bird watching.

Bashing the Boy Scouts is part of a much broader campaign against all sport fishing, and particularly tournament fishing. Specifically, bass fishing tournaments – in which fish are caught, kept in a live well for some length of time before being weighed later in the day – are condemned by animal rights activists. PETA devotes an entire section of its website to FishingHurts.com, quoting Michael W. Fox, D.V.M., Ph.D., and author of *Do Fish Have Feelings?* (see *The Animals' Agenda*, July/August 1987), "Even though fish don't scream when they are in pain and anguish, their behavior should be evidence enough of their suffering when they are hooked or netted. They struggle, endeavoring to escape and, by so doing, demonstrate they have a will to survive."

Hunters In Hiding?

Sport anglers have not reacted harshly, and in most cases, not even defensively, perhaps because most anglers remain convinced they have nothing to be concerned about. They might take a lesson from hunters, who initially thought animal rights extremists were nothing more than a handful of crackpots. Now, after years of witnessing anti-hunting demonstrations and seeing many in their ranks harassed by anti-hunters, the hunters now have a different attitude, but not exactly what one might expect from a stereotype. Political correctness has crept into the hunting ranks. Most significantly, the "K"-word has been largely replaced by "harvest." There is a great effort within the hunting community to present a more sensitive and softer image.

Some might interpret what has happened in the hunting community to be tantamount to an admission of guilt. Hunter education courses now devote much attention to the teaching of "ethics" and "wildlife management" where they originally concentrated almost entirely on firearm safety and outdoors responsibility, leaving the teaching of "ethics" to a youngster's parents and grandparents, who learned it from *their* ancestors.

Admittedly, some hunter education instructors – all unpaid and highly-dedicated volunteers – suggest that "ethics change" with the passage of time, and what might have been considered ethical by our grandparents may not be so, today. One instructor told the author in an e-mail that his father used to come back from hunting trips with deer strapped to the top of his station wagon. By today's standards, he said, that would be simply unacceptable because it could be offensive to other motorists.

New hunters are counseled that they should not display their game animals, rather hiding them from view, especially during transport, because of the potential negative public reaction. California's hunter education manual admonishes new hunters: "It is irresponsible to display your game kill to the world on top of your vehicle, or to mount its head on your bumper. This kind of behavior offends many people. Hunters need public support from people who don't hunt but do respect wildlife. Pack game home covered, wrapped, or in a closed vehicle whenever it is legal. If you want to show your harvest to your friends, do it with pictures."

The North-Central regional hunter education manual (used by several states in the Upper Midwest) cautions, "Do not put your game on top of your vehicle. This offends many people. Hunters need support from non-hunters. Cover your game. Place it in a closed vehicle if legal."

This has spread to newspapers. For example, a few years ago, the *Daily Sentinel* in Grand Junction, Colorado ran a story headlined thusly: "Don't carry your kill as a hood ornament; Public perception of hunters suffers by showoff displays."

In the early 1990s, according to the Dec. 11 issue of *High Country News*, the Colorado State University chapter of The Wildlife Society (TWS), an organization of professional wildlife biologists based in Bethesda, Maryland, insisted that hunters cover their game during transport and made a political issue of their position. They petitioned the Colorado Wildlife Commission to make concealing game mandatory. The commission decided that this practice should instead be promoted in brochures and its Hunter Education course.

Does all of this subliminally telegraph to the next generation of hunters that there may be something to be ashamed of, and something to hide, about what they are doing? Are these suggestions largely in response to the anti-hunting agenda, which has been to portray hunters as "Bambi killers," blood-thirsty louts and ignorant rednecks; an image all-too-often perpetuated by editorial cartoonists? Are they offered to project a "cleaner" image of the hunter?

Vence Malernee, a former managing editor of *Fishing & Hunting News*, once the nation's largest outdoor weekly newspaper and now an outdoor news magazine, noted, "While tasteful display of game may be a reasonable point of order, youth should be proud of what they do, and be encouraged to share the joy of the moment with fellow hunters."

A devoted deer and bird hunter, Malernee recalled how, in Durango, Colorado he would witness hunters frequently stop in supermarket parking lots to display the bucks they had killed, and nobody seemed terribly offended. Quite the opposite was actually true, he observed. Successful hunters would typically draw admiring onlookers to examine their animals.

He also noted something else: "Pride and encouragement of the new generation of hunters is the only thing we have that will not only help perpetuate the hunting tradition, but also – and more importantly – support the preservation and enhancement of our wildlife, and support the management of game. That's not only vital from the sense of man and his base instinct of survival, it is essential for the survival and expansion of wildlife populations."

As if to build on that statement, but on a slightly different plane, there are now fishing education classes, though they are somewhat disguised under the broad term of "aquatics education." Unlike with hunting, these fishing education classes are not mandatory in order for people to purchase fishing licenses and participate in the activity.

The sport fishing industry, seeing the interest in angling decline in recent years – and with that, a decline in their consumer base – has mounted an effort to attract more fishermen and women in a growing urban society. Witness the creation of the Future Fisherman Foundation, a non-profit educational arm of the American Sportfishing Association, along with programs that carry a social message, such as "Hooked on Fishing, Not on Drugs" projects conducted in cooperation with local schools, and sometimes even law enforcement agencies or other public service entities.

Such programs have had a positive benefit. They introduce a new generation to outdoor activities that otherwise might be erased from the American social landscape. In the process, they educate people about the importance of water quality and protection of marine habitat.

What would PETA have done, suggest that it might be alright to burn fish hatcheries (while rushing to the microphones to disavow personal involvement)? PETA naturally roots for the fish, but would they delight in the possibility of a fisherman getting hurt, the same as anti-hunters have occasionally suggested it would be okay for hunters to be injured or killed? That question might have already been answered by the "campaign that really wasn't." In September 2001, PETA barely started a grotesque billboard advertising campaign in Florida that asked, "Would You Give Your Right Arm to Know Why Sharks Attack, Could it be Revenge?"

The campaign was abruptly pulled after two children were attacked by sharks, one losing an arm and the other dying. One of the attacks was off shore from Pensacola, where the billboard would have been unveiled. In that attack, the shark was killed and the boy's arm retrieved and later reattached. In the other attack, a 10-year-old boy was killed off the beach near Norfolk, Virginia, where PETA's headquarters are located.

A third fatal attack, claiming the life of a 27-year-old man, occurred off North Carolina's Outer Banks.

In an attempt to justify the campaign while strategically backing out, PETA spokesman Dan Shannon noted at the time, "Our message is that humans kill billions of fish, including sharks, each year, in the most hideous ways, and sharks aren't really to blame for doing what comes naturally, because, unlike us, they don't have choices when it comes to what to eat. But right now people would just shoot the messenger without hearing the message."

Six

THE 2001 ANIMAL RIGHTS CONFERENCE

Each year, animal rights organizations from across the country gather for an annual Animal Rights Conference. These gatherings attract people representing such groups as PETA, the Animal Rights Network, Fund for Animals, National Anti-Vivisection Society, United Poultry Concerns, Physicians Committee for Responsible Medicine, Sea Shepherd International and assorted vegan organizations, along with various other left-leaning groups.

As with any other gathering that brings together like minded individuals for the purpose of discussing issues relevant to them, there is not, on the surface, anything wrong with such a conference. At past gatherings, animal rights leaders like PETA's Ingrid Newkirk have expressed support for raiding laboratories and burning them down. These conferences seem to bring out the best in some people.

What was different about the 2001 conference is that Newkirk was nowhere to be found, apparently having avoided the gathering because of in-fighting among various groups and individuals who were reportedly miffed at PETA over its media prominence. Whether this was anger over the messages, or over the contributions that they brought to PETA's coffers and nobody else's, there reportedly was quite a lot of bitterness, and Newkirk prudently stayed away.

One other difference between the 2001 convention and the others was that in the audience during those six days in the summer of 2001 was one Dr. James M. Beers, retired biologist who had served with some distinction and, ultimately, with some notoriety, in the U.S. Fish and Wildlife Service, much of that having been in law enforcement.

Beers is the biologist whose career hit a political brick wall when, in the second Clinton Administration, he went public about how the FWS, under Interior Secretary Bruce Babbitt and FWS Director Jamie Clark, both Clinton appointees, had strayed considerably from its mandate and had actually provided funds for animal rights organizations while distancing itself from fishermen, hunters and trappers.

His allegations were the foundation for a Congressional investigation by a committee chaired by Alaska Congressman Don Young.

Beers had rejected a grant application from the Fund for Animals, despite pressure by supervisors who wanted it approved. Reportedly, the Fund for Animals wanted the grant to finance the distribution of anti-hunting materials in public schools. Beers had spent 31 years in federal service for wildlife, and his career ended when he tried to stick up for the values that he had lived by throughout his professional life.

FWS first wanted to transfer Beers out of the agency headquarters in Arlington, Virginia to a regional office in Hadley, Massachusetts in February 1998. Beers declined to be transferred, arguing that it was illegal, and because the transfer was only to get him out of Arlington after he refused to approve the Fund for Animals grant application.

The next FWS move came April 14, when, according to an official document from the U.S. Office of Special Counsel (OSC), the agency "proposed to remove Mr. Beers from the federal service for failing to accept the proposed transfer." OSC asked FWS to delay that removal, and FWS waited four months before taking further action, but when the agency did act, it was dramatic.

On Aug. 21, 1998, Beers was advised in a letter from the Department of Interior that he was prohibited from entering his office facility at Arlington Square unless escorted by Bob Lange, chief of the Federal Aid Division, or the acting chief. Three days later, FWS notified Beers that the "removal action" would be effective on Aug. 28, but OSC stepped in again, telling the Interior Department that it would seek a formal stay of the removal. After some negotiating, Beers was placed on paid administrative leave.

The case dragged on for months, until finally, on April 22, 1999, OSC filed a petition for Corrective Action on behalf of Beers with the Merit Systems Protection Board against the FWS.

In June 1999, Beers finally received a settlement from the Interior Department for $150,000 plus restoration and payment of his annual leave, payment of his attorney fees, a letter from FWS apologizing for the way he was treated, and the expulsion from his files all references to his removal and a ban on his entry into his office building.

Beers had become a casualty of a political war that has erupted in recent years, and especially during the eight-year Clinton administration, as animal rights sympathizers gained positions of responsibility and helped to steer the national wildlife management agenda away from its traditional roots. His story led to an investigation by the General Accounting Office that discovered FWS money from the federal Pittman-Robertson Fund – solely raised by excise taxes on firearms, ammunition and hunting-related equipment – had been diverted to other purposes including travel to South America, Asia and Europe, and other expenses racked up by Clinton Administration bureaucrats. There was also a plan to use about $30 million from Duck Stamp revenues to purchase a Pacific atoll called Palmyra and turn it into a national wildlife refuge.

Just how serious a problem this became during the Clinton Administration may never be known. According to testimony before the House Resources Subcommittee in May, 2000 by Bonnie Kline – another FWS employee who blew the whistle – she was ordered to destroy certain FWS computer files containing sought-after details on agency spending from October 1997 through January 1998. When Kline refused, her security clearance was stripped, her safe combination was changed, she was subjected to harassment and an apparent assault attempt, and the questionable files vanished, anyway.

So outraged at all of this was the *Washington Times* that, on April 10, 2000 it published an editorial headlined "Free Bonnie Kline." In that editorial, the *Times* stated, in part:

"Miss Kline has had to endure a seemingly endless campaign of harassment and threats following her cooperation with a federal investigation of the agency…

"They contrived excuses to reprimand her and to strip her job responsibilities from her. They isolated her at a hallway desk and made not-so-veiled threats against her…

"Miss Kline said that after testifying before the Resources Committee, a fellow employee threw a telephone at her, only narrowly missing her…

Kline was evidently not injured in that attack, but incredibly, when she filed a complaint, "the U.S. government actually substituted itself for the defendant in the case on grounds that the phone thrower was acting in the performance of her duties," the newspaper stated.

The blistering *Times* editorial concluded, "An investigation by the General Accounting Office into allegations of agency waste and abuse noted that 'the combined experience of the audit team that did this work represents about 160 years worth of audit experience. To our knowledge, this is, if not the worst, one of the worst managed programs we have encountered'."

Beers testified to these abuses twice before Congress, in July and September 1999, and he became an overnight folk hero among many pro-hunting organizations.

Now an accepted authority on government shenanigans involving wildlife and allegations of mismanagement, Beers was one of the first people interviewed by the *Washington Times* when the newspaper reported a major wildlife research scandal in late 2001. Employees of FWS, the U.S. Forest Service and the Washington Department of Fish and Wildlife had apparently falsified data and evidence in the study of possible Canadian Lynx presence in national forests located in Washington state, and had concealed the problem for almost a year.

Beers told the newspaper that he was not surprised at the disclosure, and offered at the time that he believed more such situations existed for what he branded as "so-called higher purposes."

Not so coincidentally, the Vail, Colorado ski resort fire in October 1998 for which ELF had claimed credit, had apparently been set to disrupt or halt the resort's expansion of ski trails into "possible lynx habitat," the *Washington Times* reported.

So for Beers to attend an Animal Rights Conference – this one held at the Hilton Hotel in McLean, Virginia – was a remarkable turn of events, but not nearly so remarkable as what he reportedly observed and overheard while there. But the retired biologist went, following several requests from members of the Conservation Force, a conservation organization based in Louisiana and chaired by John Jackson.

In his widely-circulated report, Beers noted that Jackson "...believed that was important for hunters and other sustainable use supporters to attend this conference just as animal rights representatives attended annual wildlife management meetings." True enough, animal rights activists have attended annual conferences held by the International Association of Fish & Wildlife Agencies (IAFWA) and the Governor's Symposium on Hunting Heritage, among others. They have even been invited to the Governor's Symposium.

In his lengthy report on the Animal Rights Conference, circulated on the Internet, Beers disclosed discussions that were of a political nature that had nothing to do with animal rights but instead were geared toward a radical left political philosophy.

The Extremist Left

There is little dispute that the animal rights movement is largely populated by, and certainly linked to, radical left fringe extremists, and literature that Beers observed on tables covered the liberal landscape.

Interviewed for this book, Beers observed that the July 2001 conference brought together "a big coalition of radical leftists."

In his published report, Beers said materials were available alleging that President Bush was oppressing minorities and using religion to kill the Constitution. In addition, there were pamphlets discussing how the World Bank was buckling to protesters, asserting that chemistry is killing poor people around the world, and offering reasons why the war on drugs should be stopped.

During conversations, he also heard people suggest that

they should read the writings of Angela Davis, and "get whites upset, this energizes minorities."

Beers further noted that video presentations were constantly being played, critical of hunting and circuses, among other topics.

Perhaps what disturbed him most were comments he overheard, including discussions about how firearms must be eliminated from society, and asserting that anyone who owns a gun must only want it for the purpose of killing.

Likewise, there were discussions about tactics that work in the animal rights crusade. He quoted one individual who insisted that "There are no consequences of arrest." Another, he reported, suggested that, "Lying, cheating, destruction and 'anything else' are justified since society won't listen and the laws are against us."

Yet another individual reportedly noted that "Bomb threats at key moments in England have won the day for us."

A fourth person reportedly insisted that "White males must be suppressed."

It became clear to Beers that this was no simple animal rights conference but a convention of far-left extremists, of varying persuasions. These people had firmly gained a foothold in environmental and wildlife management affairs during the Clinton Administration. If there were any doubt, it evaporated when Beers heard speakers complain that "Clinton didn't do enough for us" while "Bush is an enemy to all of us."

High on their agenda were strategies to ban hunting, sport and commercial fishing, and trapping, and the elimination of all fish and wildlife management. They spoke about the use of economic and peer pressure, physical threats, and how far animal rights activists should go in their efforts to "liberate" animals.

During one discussion, Beers allegedly heard an unidentified university instructor note, "I've been arrested six times and I still teach at my university. Some places like San Francisco will never prosecute you for anything. Put bricks through windows to intimidate wives and children."

Pointedly, according to Beers' report, many of those in attendance were keen on gun control, discussing how guns and the oppression of women and minorities were linked. There were even representatives from NARAL, the pro-abortion organization, in attendance. Another attendee labored to show how guns create violent children and how hunter education courses turn kids into criminals, and yet another explained that to eliminate the guns, one must also eliminate hunting, or vice versa.

"These people realize," Beers reported, "that making guns unobtainable will be the death knell for hunting, trapping, and wildlife management. So they naturally and aggressively want to 'catch up' to England, Canada, Australia, the UN, and dictatorships throughout the world."

He also noted that they have established alliances and coalitions with "other radical groups that are also committed to gun control. They are working together promoting local ordinances and state and federal laws.

"There is no place for guns in the world these folks envision," Beers observed. "The sooner they eliminate the guns and gun ownership in the current world, the sooner they believe they will achieve their other goals."

Wrote Beers: "The people and groups that gathered at this luxury Hilton Hotel for five days made no bones that they are going to eliminate every traditional use of animals and many other American freedoms and traditions. They have been going about this incrementally for years. Since there have been no serious consequences of their activities, their boldness and arrogance has reached gargantuan proportions. They clearly believe and preach the radical reformation of the way we live, the way we relate to our government and the elimination of most freedoms that we take for granted here in the USA. They intend to change the relationship between mankind and the animal world that has existed for millennia."

Tactics for Victory

Beers spent enough time listening to various animal rights attendees that he was able to create an extensive log of various strategies and tactics promoted by these people. For example, they were advised to "stress issues that divide hunters…" including hunting with hounds and baiting.

Much attention was given to PETA's efforts against sport fishing (detailed in Chapter Five) with one person reportedly noting that "PETA has cracked the wholesomeness of fishing. This will deter families and help us with the wholesome labels of other animal uses."

Borrowing another page out of the PETA playbook, confrontation and intimidation of people wearing fur, including fur collars, was advocated. This includes attempts to embarrass people wearing fur in front of their friends. Likewise, tactics that put fur stores out of business were promoted.

On dealing with politicians, it was noted that anything goes. Animal rights advocates also seemed proud of their connections in Congress, specifically Senators Jim Jeffords (I-VT) and Bob Smith (R-NH) identified as "two of our best friends."

At least one speaker gloated about how the animal rights movement has "eliminated several enemies like Slade Gorton (R-WA)."

At one point, according to Beers' account, a speaker

suggested that "Eighty percent of the people are assholes."

State agencies were also characterized as "enemies" of the animal rights movement. At one point, Beers wrote, a speaker said federal controls "break the back of state fish and wildlife agencies that are pro-hunting."

Beers, in his concluding remarks, noted that "the leaders and lawyers" made it a point to avoid "the more explosive sessions."

Infiltrating Government

Beers spent the final years of his career with FWS as a representative of state fish and wildlife agencies on an international scale dealing with wildlife issues. He told the author that his travels took him to Europe, where he was involved in efforts to prevent European nations from banning the importation of furs.

"They would have dealt a death blow to trapping and fur farming in Russia, Canada and the United States," he explained. "PETA was pretty active, and I was never a big compromiser, always a fighter."

He said representatives from PETA and other animal rights groups would frequently appear at such conferences, and endeavor to be included in work groups and committees. This activism extends to the United Nations, where he said animal rights activists have consistently tried for inclusion.

While there may be nothing fundamentally wrong with that – if one considers that every interest has a right to be heard – Beers said his resistance to the animal rights philosophy during meetings and conferences had an unpleasant "side effect."

"I used to get all kinds of threats here at home," he said. "I've been threatened on my phone."

At one point, he said, someone tried to run him off the road, an incident he never reported to police.

"I don't want to identify myself to police as making claims about things that I am not able to prove," he explained.

All of that considered, Beers is very concerned about invitations extended to PETA and other animal rights groups to attend wildlife management conferences. He disdained the motives of conference organizers who would, for example, ask Newkirk or other high-profile animal rights activists participate in panel discussions.

"They want to project an image to the public that they are trying to reach out," he said.

In fairness, it must be noted that the Governor's Symposium also invited rock singer Ted Nugent, an avowed hunter and author of *Kill It and Grill It*. A member of the National Rifle Association Board of Directors, Nugent represents everything animal rights extremists love to hate.

Beers alleged that the apparent concern among the administrators and biologists hosting those events is to continue to justify the existence of their jobs in the event hunting and fishing falls by the wayside or is outlawed. There is a major problem with that philosophy, he stressed.

"The system will collapse if you do away with Pittman-Robertson and Dingell-Johnson money and license revenues," he said, "but nobody wants to admit that."

Pittman-Robertson and Dingell-Johnson refer to the special federal excise taxes on hunting and fishing equipment, respectively. Revenues from these taxes are apportioned to the states for fish and wildlife restoration and enhancement programs. Up to ten percent of the Pittman-Robertson funds may be used to support hunter education programs and shooting range development. The money is administered by FWS's office of Federal Aid, where Beers was working when his troubles began with that agency in 1998.

Beers contended that some state resources agencies are now staffed with, or influenced so heavily by, non-hunters, and possibly even anti-hunters, that "they are committed to getting out of hunting and fishing." But the self-destructive catch to that would be the loss in justification to have a fish and wildlife agency if there is no fishing or hunting, he argued.

The loss of such agencies is of no great concern to animal rights extremists, of course. Their ultimate goal is to eliminate hunting and fishing, and they gather at their annual conferences to develop methods to accomplish that goal.

Asked straight away whether he thinks PETA is a "dangerous organization," Beers' response was equally blunt.

"Without a doubt! That's like asking me if the sun is going to come up in the morning," he replied.

He said PETA is "an activist/demonstration-oriented" organization.

"If you feel romantic about wildlife and saving the world," Beers observed, "PETA is the first group that comes to mind. A lot of people looking for a cause gravitate towards PETA."

He said PETA attracts people looking for a way to channel their activism – regardless what they feel "active" about – and such people are easily recruited for anti-hunting or anti-fur demonstrations. Some of these individuals, he said, find their way to other groups, where they participate in the kind of criminal activities for which ALF and ELF have become infamous.

Specifically regarding the 2001 Animal Rights Conference, Beers noted that many of those in attendance had crossed state lines for the expressed purpose of networking with other activists to plan or promote illegal activities. That, he indicated, could be considered a criminal act in itself.

"The FBI should have been in there arresting people," he said.

Seven

DANGEROUSLY
DISINGENUOUS

Incorporated in the state of Delaware in the summer of 1980, People for the Ethical Treatment of Animals has been described by Dr. Edward Taub as "dangerous and extremely malicious."

Author Ron Arnold, executive vice president of the Center for Defense of Free Enterprise, says PETA is "extremely litigious." They have, for example, a well-established history of legal warfare with circus operations. Perhaps the most astonishing lawsuit of all, though, was mounted in mid-2002 when PETA announced it was suing officials at Ringling Bros. and Barnum & Bailey Circus for spying on PETA operations by hiring a former top CIA operative.

Contrast astonishing with downright ludicrous, and you get the lawsuit PETA filed against New Jersey's Department of Environmental Protection's Fish and Wildlife Division for that November 2001 turnpike collision with the deer.

The animal rights movement has attracted an assortment of characters who have a keenly-developed talent for playing word games, and nobody has played them better than PETA founders Alex Pacheco and Ingrid Newkirk, "suggesting" or "promoting" certain activities while claiming not to actually "endorse" those activities or actually participate in any of them.

Yet many of these people do not seem to remember from one day to the next, or from one public statement to another, where they have drawn the line.

When it comes to being disingenuous, Newkirk is a sage practitioner. In a Nov. 5, 2001 commentary she wrote for CNSNews.com called *PETA 'Terra-ists,'* Newkirk proclaimed, "PETA does not condone...violent acts."

Then why has Newkirk suggested – as she did at the 1997 animal rights convention – that it would be okay to burn labs?

In the same article, Newkirk stated, "We value animal life..." and later added, "Who is really more violent? The people who imprison animals...and deliberately ...Kill them...?"

Is that the same Ingrid Newkirk, PETA president, who advised Dr. William M. Sims, Jr. with the Virginia Department of Agriculture and Consumer Services' Division of Animal Industry Services that, during 2001, the organization's animal shelter euthanized (that's a polite term for "killed") 310 dogs, 1,601 cats, 29 "other companion animals," and four birds, a total of 1,944 animals?

According to photocopies of documents submitted to the Virginia agency and obtained by the author under the Freedom of Information Act, during a five-month period from July 1 through Dec. 31, 1998, PETA euthanized 68 of 90 wild animals turned over to its care, along with 124 of the 210 dogs, 533 of the 793 cats, and 28 of the 35 "other companion animals.

That's a lot of killing for an organization that "values animal life." And it perhaps explains the double standard philosophy under which PETA seems to operate; it's okay for animal rights zealots to take an animal's life, but not okay for a hunter, cattle rancher, poultry farmer or even a sport angler.

Endorsing Killers

Whether one has blood on his own hands, or simply kills by proxy, the victim is none the less dead. This is the philosophy that has guided the Ingrid Newkirks and Alex Pachecos of the world to promote vegan diets and disdain those who eat meat, even if they do not hunt and only get their steaks from a grocery store or butcher shop.

The same disdain never seems to get directed inward. Otherwise, PETA might have to renounce its own Dan Mathews, who told *Genre* magazine for its December/January 2000 issue that he admired serial killer Andrew Cunanan. His reason: "Because he got Versace to stop doing fur."

Gianni Versace was the famous clothing designer who was gunned down July 15, 1997 outside his Florida home. The gun Cunanan used was the same pistol he had used in two other homicides, in Minnesota.

Then there was PETA's irrepressible Buckingham Palace streaker Bruce Friedrich who extolled Oklahoma City bomber Timothy McVeigh's virtues for having a meat-free last meal.

What about when nobody is killed, but only property is damaged or destroyed? Newkirk is up there leading the charge with her book *Free The Animals*, pandered as the true story of the Animal Liberation Front. Why does Newkirk, who does not "endorse" violence, suggest in her author's note: "Determined to cause economic injury to the exploiters, ALF members burn down their emptied buildings and smash their vehicles to smithereens. Perhaps after reading this book, you will find that you cannot blame them."

What about these terrorists that Newkirk and PETA endorses? What does this say about Newkirk and her organization?

ALF spokesman David Barbarash has been rather disingenuous in his own right, once insisting in an Oct. 24, 1999 ALF press release, "We do not consider the destruction of property, of things, to be committing violence. How does one commit violence against something which is not alive?"

Then comes ALF's Katie Fedor, quoted by the Associated Press after the $12 million October 1998 arson at Vail, Colorado for which the Earth Liberation Front took credit, stating, "It's a war. It's a nonviolent revolution. Unfortunately, the traditional routes to societal change such as lobbying haven't worked. Constituents are not being heard. We are forced to take nonviolent action."

Remember, ALF does not consider destruction of property to be violent, so it couches its remarks, at least some of the time. That is not always the case, as with Ronnie Lee, ALF founder and once its spokesman (now reportedly "retired"). When he was quoted by the London *Daily Telegraph* on Feb. 24, 2001 discussing the attack on Brian Cass, manager of the Huntingdon Life Sciences (see Chapter Four), Lee observed, "This serves Brian Cass right and is totally justifiable. In fact, he got off lightly. I have no sympathy for him. I do not condemn this act..."

Cass could easily have been killed in that attack. That prospect did not seem to bother Lee. Would it have truly bothered anyone at PETA? Perhaps the answer to that question lies in the amount of money PETA has provided to ALF associates over the years.

Hiring Criminals

PETA will probably never approach the Salvation Army in terms of providing opportunities for the people society leaves behind. In PETA's case, it has provided employment for some people society might be better off without.

Of course, publicly PETA would never endorse any criminal act, but one must temper that with a careful look at those to whom PETA provides a home, or at least has assisted in the past.

And remember one very important fact: Your typical animal rights activist does not, and probably never will, consider someone a "criminal" in the legal or moral sense if that individual was arrested and jailed for committing an act in the cause of animal rights.

Rodney Coronado and Roger Troen are just two of the recipients of PETA's benevolence, and they were never even on the payroll. That has not always been the case with animal rights zealots who had criminal histories.

One such individual would be Timothy Andrew Ray of Norfolk, Virginia. Here is yet another example of PETA saying one thing, then having to acknowledge something else.

On June 10, 1999 following a demonstration against the World Pork Expo in Des Moines, Iowa, Ray was arrested on the steps of the Iowa capitol building for allegedly setting fire to several bales of hay that were part of the protest. At the time, PETA spokeswoman Dawn Carr claimed the fire had not been planned as part of the protest and, besides, she insisted she did not know Ray.

Carr – another PETA staffer with a police record and court conviction – will be remembered as the woman who threw a pie in the face of Brandy DeJongh, after the 21-year-old Miss DeJongh had just been crowned Miss Rodeo America during ceremonies in Las Vegas, Nevada. In December 2000, Carr pleaded guilty to misdemeanor battery and received a year's probation for the offense. She also had to pay $1,700 for damages to DeJongh's dress.

When quizzed about the Des Moines fire, Carr reportedly stated, "We were just out there doing our thing with the dancing pig when this guy ran up and tried to set the hay on fire."

"This guy" happened to be Ray, who coincidentally had been a vegan activist in St. Louis and had just moved from there to Norfolk to take a job with PETA as a "campaign staffer." On the following day, who should show up to bail Ray out of jail but Dawn Carr, posting a $6,500 cash bond against the $32,500 bail.

But Carr and Ray simply do not hold a candle to ex-teacher Gary Yourofsky. Formerly a teacher in Detroit, Michigan Yourofsky is unquestionably one of Michigan's most vocal and notorious animal rights activists.

Yourofsky is the founder of Animals Deserve Absolute Protection Today and Tomorrow (ADAPTT), another animal rights organization. It is based in Royal Oak, Michigan with a contact in Florida. Michigan residents may recall the advertising campaign sponsored by ADAPTT that attacked "animal slavery" of circuses which aired on television. That campaign was funded by a $10,000 grant from PETA.

He has racked up a rather impressive list of animal rights misadventures, some of which have landed him in jail. The most infamous of these was his participation in an April 1997 fur farm raid near Blenheim, Ontario which earned him a six-month prison sentence, though he eventually only served 77 days of that. He went on a hunger strike immediately after being sentenced.

One wonders whether the hunger strike was to protest his incarceration, or being sold out by his uncle, Alan Hoffman, who had also gone on the raid along with three women identified as Hilma Ruby, Robyn Weiner and Patricia Dodson. In that raid, Yourofsky opened over 1,500 cages. He and his uncle had gone back to Blenheim and taken a cab, and were quickly stopped by police who found them reportedly covered with mink fur and feces.

Allegedly faced with the unsettling prospect of tough Canadian justice, Hoffman and Weiner made statements against Yourofsky in exchange for lighter sentences. This was apparently a precedent, as acknowledged on ADAPTT's own website in a lengthy introductory piece about Yourofsky, in which it was noted that Hoffman and Weiner "broke the code of the animal liberation movement: never tell on another."

Doesn't that sound like the code of another interesting organization with a long history of activity in the United States…the Mafia?

Ironically, it was reported that most of the minks turned loose by Yourofsky that Easter night perished as a result.

In August 1999, Yourofsky was back in the news – and in jail – after chaining himself underneath his automobile to block access to the Detroit Animal Control Center.

Other than getting money from PETA for the advertisement, ADAPTT has apparently not been much of a growing concern despite Yourofsky's claim of over 2,000 members, because in early 2002, he was forced to lament in an open letter that, after "sixty-six months of working for NO PAY," he was stepping down from his position as ADAPTT president to get a job and pay off his bills.

Within two months, Yourofsky breathlessly announced in another open letter that he had gotten a great job offer…from Ingrid Newkirk. He described this resurrection thusly: "The day after my resignation letter was sent out a couple of months ago, I received a phone call from Ingrid Newkirk, PETA's founder and president…Ingrid's message was touching and emotional, to say the least. Frankly, I was blown away that Ingrid would call me with concern because I could no longer continue my activism. Getting a call and/or a request from Ingrid is like getting a call from the Godfather's Don Corleone. It's an offer one can't refuse." What was that about the code of the Mafia?

As of May 20, 2002 Yourofsky had been hired as PETA's "national lecturer." And just where are these lectures to occur?

According to Yourofsky's open letter, "(O)ur goal is to have DAILY lectures set up in schools across the U.S. when the fall semester begins next September." One can only wonder how that will square with school officials who practice a "zero tolerance" policy toward youngsters who bring toy guns, pocket knives or even play school yard shoot-'em-up using their fingers as play guns. After all, when Yourofsky was interviewed by *Toledo Blade* writer Jack Lessenberry in mid-2001, he was asked whether it would be acceptable for someone to kill an "animal abuser."

"I would unequivocally support that, too," Yourofsky told the columnist.

So, while Newkirk travels around the country carefully declining to directly endorse violence, she hires someone who is not so shy about it to deliver lectures in public schools to impressionable youngsters.

This becomes all the more curious when one considers what Yourofsky has confessed about himself in his interview with the *Blade's* Lessenberry: "I don't even like most animals."

Promoting Crimes?

PETA not only is disingenuous about insisting that it does not endorse crime. It also rabidly insists that it does not promote criminal acts.

The argument apparently fell on deaf ears in the United Kingdom early in 2002 when PETA had planned to sponsor an advertisement to run in movie theaters (that's "cinemas" in Great Britain) that was simply too harsh for the Cinema Advertising Association (CAA) to stomach.

The advertisement in question was reportedly filmed in Dublin, Ireland and had originally been planned for distribution to American theaters in November 2001. However, that plan was derailed by the Sept. 11, 2001 terrorist attacks on New York and Washington, D.C. because, according to a story on Ananova, it was "deemed too graphic for an audience already traumatized" by the terrorist outrage.

Apparently, PETA did not expect the British to have been quite so "traumatized," so the plan was to begin showing the advertisement there in late winter and early spring.

What was so offensive about this advertisement? You be the judge.

The sequence opened with a well-dressed, attractive woman strolling through a shopping mall. She is suddenly attacked and beaten to the ground, presumably left lying dead, by a man who steals the fur coat she is wearing. As the darkly-clad, crew cut man strolls away with the coat held tightly in his arms, the advertisement inquires: "What if you were killed for your coat?"

When first interviewed about the advertisement, an unidentified PETA spokesman told Ananova that fur had been in the headlines recently, especially in the aftermath of model Cindy Crawford's appearance at a Milan fashion show, "...so we've decided to seize the initiative and launch this campaign early."

When the British CAA blocked the advertisement from running in any theater in the country, PETA's spokesman then told Ananova: "We wanted people to be alarmed when they see the advert (sic) because the treatment of animals is more than alarming. We want people to imagine being in the same position as the model in the advert or an animal, killed for its coat."

One might reasonably ask how PETA could simply suggest that this advertisement was designed just to make people "think" considering some of the past activities in which PETA staffers and sympathizers, and other animal rights "activists" went considerably farther than just thinking.

Don't think it's possible? You don't think it's not that great a leap from expressing no serious alarm at the potential killing of an "animal abuser" to the point where someone actually does it? Explain that disbelief to the family, friends and followers of Dutch politician Pim Fortuyn, an admitted gay and flamboyant political activist who wanted to be prime minister of the Netherlands. In early May 2002, in the midst of a campaign for the Dutch Parliament, Fortuyn was gunned down, allegedly by a suspect identified as an "animal rights and environmental activist" named Volkert Van der Graaf.

Van der Graaf was chased down and captured a short distance away, gun in hand.   Fortuyn had disdained the environmental movement and had also suggested that, if elected, he might work to end a ban on breeding animals for fur. His was the first political assassination in the Netherlands in 350 years.

In the wake of his murder, Dutch authorities began looking at Van der Graaf as a possible suspect in the 1996 murder of Chris Van de Werken, an environmental officer. That killing was reportedly very much like the Fortuyn slaying. Both shootings were at close range, and both men were reportedly killed with the same caliber handgun and the same ammunition: Silver Tip hollow points. The only known maker of such ammunition is Winchester/Olin, and that ammunition is reportedly rarely available in The Netherlands.

The Fortuyn assassination was "meticulously planned" according to various news agencies. When Dutch police searched Van der Graff's residence, they found not only a trove of animal rights and environmental literature, they also found detailed maps of the location where the killing occurred.

Though animal rights organizations set speed records in trying to distance themselves from the suspect, he was widely identified as a member of the group Environmental Offensive. According to the *Sunday Times* of London, Van der Graaf had been active in the animal rights movement since he was a teenager.

There is no known connection, financial or otherwise, between Van der Graaf and any American animal rights organization.

However, it was worthy enough for the *Sunday Times* to note that an animal rights group Van der Graaf founded as a teenager was called the Zeeland Animal Liberation Front.

Eight

PETA'S ROKKE
ROAD IN COURT

Michelle Rokke is either a heroine or villain, depending upon one's point of view, but it might be easily argued that it was her undercover activities that were the catalyst for two major legal actions against People for the Ethical Treatment of Animals that perhaps caused the animal rights organization to take the proverbial step back and pause for a deep breath. Then again, probably not.

In June 1996, according to various accounts researched for this book, Rokke – who had once reportedly worked in Rochester, Minnesota as a hairdresser and, in relation to her "undercover investigations," was identified as a "PETA activist" – took a job at the Village Veterinary Hospital of Dr. Howard Baker in East Brunswick, New Jersey. As she would later testify under cross-examination in court, when filling out her job application and detailing her employment background, Rokke carefully neglected to mention that she was employed by PETA.

It was not the first time Rokke had done an "undercover assignment" and her activities in the Baker case were reminiscent of the 1981 incident involving PETA founder Alex Pacheco going to work for Dr. Edward Taub at Silver Springs, Maryland in preparation for the monkey caper discussed earlier.

By no odd coincidence, that same month, Rokke had also applied for a job with Huntingdon Life Sciences in East Millstone, New Jersey, a subsidiary of the laboratory facility in Great Britain that had been the target of animal rights demonstrations and at least one physical attack, mentioned in earlier chapters. In later court testimony, Rokke would assert that she applied for the job with Baker while waiting for the Huntingdon job to open up, which it did in September of that year. She also later claimed that during the first week she worked for Baker, she saw him engage in cruelty against an animal under his care, and she had witnessed him abusing various dogs and cats. Yet Rokke continued to work for Baker until April 1997 – a full ten months – even though she had started working for Huntingdon.

While Rokke later asserted that she wanted to work for Baker to learn about working with animals (the same excuse offered by Pacheco after the Silver Springs affair), and to become an "animal caretaker" at the Huntingdon facility, it is now evident that her motives were far more intense, if not outright sinister. For, while she was working at both jobs, Rokke surreptitiously recorded hundreds of hours of activities on videotape inside both facilities using a hidden camera either in her bag or concealed in her glasses, and subsequently was accused of stealing over 8,000 documents from Huntingdon. Those documents included the company's client list and, reportedly, many of Huntingdon's trade secrets, test protocols and data related to testing, and internal memoranda.

Out of these hours upon hours of secretly-recorded tapes made at Baker's clinic – many of which were subsequently erased or lost because they were recorded over – PETA selected about three minutes of video which showed the veterinarian working with a particular dog, and sent it to the news media with allegations of animal cruelty. For Dr. Baker, it was the beginning of nearly three years of hell.

The particular three minutes of video contains audio of Baker making remarks and striking the dog, a Dalmatian, at least once. To the casual observer, it was a rather traumatic piece of "evidence."

In June 1997, two months after Rokke left Baker's employment, charges of animal cruelty were filed against Dr. Baker. His case would not come to trial for almost two years, and his final vindication nearly nine months after that.

Meanwhile, a month after Rokke left Baker's clinic and her incriminating videotape had been released to the press, her months of handiwork relating to Huntingdon leaped into the spotlight as well. In May 1997, nearly nine months after Rokke began working there, PETA began a campaign against the laboratory, alleging that canines used in tests for Colgate-Palmolive – one of its many corporate clients – had been mistreated during testing of an anti-bacterial substance the company was planning to add to its toothpaste formula.

Rokke had apparently limited her videotaping inside the Huntingdon lab to only about 50 hours, along with which were recorded at least four 90-minute audiotapes. Add that to the documents she stole, and this effort had the potential of seriously damaging, if not completely destroying, the work being conducted and the client base upon which Huntingdon depended for its business. Of course, that was PETA's intent all along.

Black Bag Specialist

Her usefulness as an undercover operator now probably non-existent, Michelle Rokke in the mid-1990s appears to have been PETA's "black bag operations specialist." Translation: She was making at least part of her living by infiltrating companies or institutions and working undercover to "get the goods" on these targets. Just how reliable were the "goods" she got remains a matter of some argument, though one court appeal, one out-of-court settlement and a trio of lengthy investigations – involving separate cases – all tend to cast serious doubt upon her, and PETA, in terms of credibility.

Rokke's work first gained prominence on Aug. 14, 1996 when PETA launched an attack on Boys Town in Omaha, Nebraska. Made famous by the Spencer Tracy movie in the 1930s, Boys Town has become something quite larger than a home for troubled boys.

Today, the facility includes a national research hospital, where all kinds of research is conducted. A husband-wife team, Drs. Edward Walsh and JoAnn McGee, had been conducting research on congenital deafness, using cats in their experiments.

Enter Rokke with hidden camera and sticky fingers to make secret videos and remove documents, later used to allege that Walsh and McGee had mistreated kittens during their hearing experiments. PETA held a press conference that warm August day across the street from Boys Town, and also filed complaints against the institution with the Department of Agriculture and the National Institutes of Health (NIH).

What ensued in the Boys Town case was a 13-month investigation by the NIH, the Agriculture Department and an independent committee appointed by the Boys Town administration. During that period, McGee and Walsh reportedly received threatening telephone calls at their offices and home, and also got some intimidating mail.

A rather detailed account of this campaign was reported in the March 24, 1998 issue of the *New York Times*, in which the newspaper quoted one such letter: "We will kill you and every member of your family in the exact same way you killed the cats. No matter where you hide! We will slice open your heads and cut the nerves in your brains while you are alive." The *Times* article dutifully noted that PETA's Ingrid Newkirk denied any responsibility for that or any other threatening letter or telephone call.

Rokke had also been busily involved in another "undercover" PETA campaign, this one against horse farms which gathered urine from the animals for use in pharmaceutical production of Premarin. According to the website, Premarin.org, Premarin is "a drug made up of conjugated estrogens obtained from the urine of pregnant mares – produced in many forms (pills, creams, injections, patches) and is used to reduce the symptoms of menopause in women or women who have had a hysterectomy. It is also prescribed to nearly eliminate the risk of osteoporosis (the brittling of bones) and reduce the chance of heart disease in women over 50."

At the end of the Boys Town investigations, all three groups – independent of one another, remember – concluded that animals had not been mistreated at the research hospital.

Huntingdon Fights Back

Obviously cognizant of the history between PETA and Huntingdon's parent facility in England, Alan Staple, president of Huntingdon's New Jersey operation, may have surprised the animal rights activists. Instead of passively trying to conduct business and leave dealing with PETA to the authorities, he fought back.

There was something worth fighting for, too. PETA's allegations against Huntingdon had cost the company over half of its clients, amounting to an estimated $1 million in lost business. Huntingdon had over 200 employees, but Staples did not reduce his work force.

Huntingdon filed a civil lawsuit against PETA using a

somewhat obscure, but devastating, section of the federal Racketeering Influenced Corrupt Organization (RICO) Act. Suddenly, here was a PETA target that was willing to compare PETA's actions to those of thieves and thugs.

The lawsuit accused PETA of engaging in a pattern of criminal behavior in its attacks on Huntingdon. Over and above the threats and harassing mail and telephone calls were Rokke's clandestine activities, which cut right to the heart of the company's case against her, individually. She had, said Huntingdon, deliberately falsified information on employment applications and deliberately violated terms of an agreement she signed that bound her to confidentiality. In Huntingdon's eyes, Rokke had violated the federal Animal Enterprise Protection and Economic Espionage acts, and had essentially perjured herself by signing a statement that all the information on her employment application was true.

The agreement Rokke had signed prohibited her from disclosing proprietary information about the company or removing any such information from the Huntingdon facility. It also prevented her from using such information for her own benefit or that of another party.

Huntingdon's lawsuit effort scored a quick point when U.S. District Judge Rebecca Beach Smith of the U.S. District Court, Eastern District in Norfolk, Virginia issued a temporary restraining order against PETA. This order prevented the animal rights group from disseminating any more of the material it had obtained during Rokke's "undercover investigation."

Naturally, Huntingdon did not stop there, for in life, there are points one reaches when there is simply no turning back from an action taken or initiated. In this particular case – to Huntingdon's credit – enough was enough, and the sort of conduct in which PETA had engaged to create trouble for the laboratory needed to be stopped.

After all, PETA had gone to the Cincinnati, Ohio head-quarters of Proctor & Gamble to hold a press conference, release its Huntingdon video and threaten the company if it continued doing business with the laboratory.

PETA, evidently using the purloined client list, allegedly began harassing some of those clients. Huntingdon contended in its lawsuit that PETA had "knowingly received possession of...stolen property from Rokke" and used that information and material to damage the company.

Pressing its case as a RICO civil offense, Huntingdon's lawsuit asserted that PETA and Rokke had conspired to steal the company materials. "Conspiracy" in a legal and criminal sense is not a good term when it is used against you.

One Settlement, One Acquittal

The Huntingdon case continued to move forward for several months, until Dec. 17, 1997, when it was announced that the laboratory and PETA had reached an out-of-court settlement.

The 15-page settlement was approved by U.S. District Court Judge Henry Morgan, and it barred PETA from mounting any undercover operation against Huntingdon for five years, and it permanently enjoined PETA from using any of the materials taken from the laboratory by Rokke.

Further, PETA was prohibited from further interfering with any of Huntingdon's relationships with its business clients. PETA had to return or destroy all the stolen documents, and turn over to Huntingdon all the video and audio tapes Rokke had recorded.

What was PETA's part of the bargain? All charges against Newkirk, Rokke and Sweetland, including the federal racketeering counts, were dropped.

Defiantly, Newkirk and PETA quickly declared a "victory," and she issued a not-too-veiled threat to fur industry groups that had supported the laboratory's legal efforts, warning them that PETA's "investigations" would not be stopped.

Quoted by the *New York Times,* Newkirk made a statement that seemed rather unusual: "Only fools litigate."

(Newkirk may one day have to explain why, if that's true, PETA was pretty quick on the legal trigger to sue ultra-liberal afternoon talk hostess Rosie O'Donnell when she made an off-the-cuff, but on-the-air remark about "PETA-approved leather." PETA's lawsuit was for $350,000 and demanded an on-air apology. O'Donnell eventually did apologize for the remark.

And Newkirk will have to account for why, if only fools litigate, PETA was equally swift in filing suit against Michael Doughney, creator of the peta.org parody website. Showing no sense of humor at all, PETA went after Doughney with a passion because in his dictionary, "PETA" stands for "People Eating Tasty Animals."

A federal appeals court ultimately ruled in PETA's favor, but nixed PETA's effort to collect $300,000 in attorneys fees and court costs. Doughney was nicked for a relatively small sum of $28,671, and as such cases often go, the furor created by the lawsuit brought huge attention to Doughney's site and his biting sense of humor. Today, references to "People Eating Tasty Animals" are frequently heard on talk radio, and are well-accepted among hunters and ranchers. Go figure.

That aside, PETA has a reputation for filing lawsuits, so if only fools litigate, someone may one day be compelled to ask Newkirk for her definition of "fool.")

While Huntingdon settled its case rather quickly against

PETA – and one is compelled to wonder whether that quick agreement had anything to do with the fact that PETA staffers were facing RICO charges – the case against Dr. Baker dragged on for well over a year beyond Huntingdon's settlement was announced.

Nineteen months later, on July 12, 1999, after a court trial during which the defense effectively destroyed the credibility of activist Rokke, Dr. Baker was nevertheless convicted on 14 counts of animal cruelty by trial judge Emery Z. Toth in Old Bridge Municipal Court in East Brunswick, N.J. Judge Toth amazingly had ruled Rokke to be a credible witness.

This must have come as a surprise to Baker and his attorney, Michael Rosenbaum, a partner in the Short Hills, New Jersey firm of Budd Larner. Rosenbaum had, through cross-examination, gotten Rokke to admit under oath that she had been deceptive when filling out her job applications, both for Dr. Baker and for Huntingdon. That was not the only point upon which Rosenbaum dismantled Rokke's veracity, it would seem.

Columnist and PETA watchdog Brian Carnell quoted from the trial transcript in a May 20, 2001 column appearing on AnimalRights.net. Rokke's responses are rather revealing.

Under cross examination, Rosenbaum – after showing Rokke a photograph of a male horse that had been used in a PETA publication to illustrate a story regarding another of Rokke's investigations, that one about pregnant mares used in the production of the drug Premarin – asked Rokke if she thought using that photo was misleading.

Rokke's response: "I don't think it was, because if you have a lot of pregnant mares, you obviously have male horses, so their care and treatment came into play as well."

Rosenbaum also asked Rokke if she had broken the

law during her time at the Huntingdon laboratory, when she stole the documents.

Since the charges against her had been dropped by then as part of the Huntingdon agreement, she replied, "Well, I'm not certain that I've broken the law, to be perfectly honest with you. You know, I've not been held up on trial in a court of law as a criminal, so no, I don't think I'm a criminal."

To which Rosenbaum responded: "Stealing company records? Stealing client lists? Stealing trade secrets? Disseminating that information?"

Rokke's reply to that, as reported by Carnell: "Well, I – I certainly don't think of myself as a criminal, no."

Judge Toth's guilty verdict was quickly appealed, and the appeals process was surprisingly speedy, considering how long appeals sometimes take. Meanwhile, Dr. Baker's veterinary license was revoked by the New Jersey Board of Veterinary Medical Examiners.

The case went before New Brunswick Superior Court Judge Joyce Munkacsi, and on April 14, 2000 she delivered a verdict that was as much a slap at the trial judge as it was at PETA and Rokke. In her reversal, and acquittal of Dr. Baker on all charges, Judge Munkacsi wrote, in part, "I cannot find Michelle Rokke to be a credible witness such as to be the reed on which the state has built this case."

The judge continued: "She (Rokke) has made a career of her devotion not to animal welfare but to animal rights. She has no training in veterinarian (sic) medicine nor any experience…Yet within two days of becoming employed by Dr. Baker, she finds abuse…"

It took less than two weeks for the New Jersey Board of Veterinary Medical Examiners to reinstate Dr. Baker's veterinary license, but the case had devastated him. Interviewed for this book, Dr. Baker told the author, "They severely hurt my reputation and they damaged my practice."

Before and during the trial, Baker received telephone and mail death threats directed against himself and his family, and his clinic was picketed. It was an ordeal for which there could only be one recourse: in late November 2000, Dr. Baker sued PETA for defamation. As this book was being written, that civil case was still in the deposition stage and no trial date had been set. Dr. Baker is still represented by the Budd Larner law firm.

Baker told the author matter-of-factly, "I have no other choice. They ruined my ability to earn a living and they destroyed my good name."

He acknowledges that he "will never be able to regain the practice I had." Yet, he said that "we feel that every day in the practice" is one more step back from the horrible ordeal through which he was put.

Pattern of Thuggery

Hate mail and death threats, harassing telephone calls at all hours of the day or night, demonstrations in front of businesses, harassment of clients; all of these are earmarks of the extremist animal rights movement.

It would be impossible to prove, and ludicrous to even suggest, that such a pattern of thuggery was specifically and solely coordinated by PETA against its targets. No doubt that some extremists, perhaps motivated by PETA accusations against certain businesses or individuals, take it upon themselves to act. Whether such action is condoned is certainly a matter for some discussion, based on statements made by Ingrid Newkirk from time to time.

Dr. Howard Baker, now acquitted and trying to resume his life and career, received numerous threats. Huntingdon Life Sciences employees have been harassed, here and in

England, and its president, Alan Staple, had been threatened with death. Other scientists and researchers have received "razor letters" in the mail, and have likewise been threatened. Universities have been firebombed. Fur farmers have been threatened, had their property destroyed and had their customers picketed. Fur retailers have been picketed, their customers harassed and occasionally assaulted by having blood (real or imitation) spattered on their garments. And so it goes.

It is this kind of conduct that reflects upon what otherwise might be acceptable as legitimate investigative work by a special interest organization that claims to be working for the welfare of animals. More importantly, as the public becomes more aware of such activities in support of the animal rights agenda, it becomes less sympathetic toward the activists-turned-extremists who plan, promote and participate in such activities.

Particularly questionable are such "hidden camera investigations" conducted clandestinely by people like Rokke. Even when major news organizations do these investigations, there is growing public skepticism about the credibility of such reports, many of which have subsequently been shown to be riddled with bias. Thousands of feet and hours of film footage are edited down to what amount to "sound bites" that may be selectively used to bolster a certain perspective, while other footage that either does not support, or possibly refutes, that perspective is discarded or destroyed. Throw in the additional element of a partisan organization doing the undercover work, and you have the formula for media and legal demagoguery.

Is this what happens with PETA investigations? That is certainly a question being asked of the courts, if not in documents, certainly by inference.

In Baker's pending litigation, he could point to the appellate court ruling to reasonably argue that Rokke used admittedly edited videotape – a few minutes out of a reported 200 hours worth of recordings, some of which had been erased or taped over with different footage – to create a false impression of what occurred at his clinic during the time she was employed there. Regardless how the Baker case is concluded, if it goes to trial or is settled out of court like the Huntingdon case, PETA may have more of a liability than an asset in associating with individuals like Rokke.

Describing Rokke in the lawsuit, Baker alleges, "Indeed, her Machiavellian devotion to her extremist cause is so compelling that she will do whatever she feels necessary, even lie, steal, withhold evidence, in her misguided zeal to protect animals from what she perceives, or more likely misperceives, to be abuse."

In an interview published in the *Bergen Record* on Nov. 24, 2000, Rokke was defiant. She was quoted by reporter Mitchel Maddux insisting, "I did nothing wrong. I reported what was a clear violation of the New Jersey cruelty law, and I'm more than happy to have the courts reexamine this case."

PETA's director of research and investigations, Mary Beth Sweetland, was equally obstreperous, telling Maddux in for the same article that Baker had been found guilty and that the verdict was correct. She contended that he "got lucky on appeal," and insisted that if the veterinarian wants to have the covertly-recorded tapes played again in court, "that's fine with us."

Because the RICO allegations were dropped as part of the Huntingdon settlement, there is certainly room for PETA to claim no wrongdoing, because nobody was ever convicted of a crime. No such charges have been brought as part of Baker's complaint, so Rokke, last reportedly working with another animal rights group in New Mexico, can argue she was acting properly, in the interest of animals.

But the "undercover investigation" is a favorite PETA tactic, and Newkirk, in the wake of the Huntingdon settlement, declared that nobody is really safe from future actions. Whether Rokke will be involved remains to be seen. (In a recent "undercover" investigation resulting in a PETA complaint against the use of laboratory rats by the University of North Carolina, the operative was identified as "activist Kate Turlington.") After all the exposure Rokke has received, one would suspect that her name is rather well circulated throughout the animal research, and perhaps even the veterinary communities. There is, of course, nothing to stop Rokke from applying for a job under an assumed name, and it could be argued, thanks to her own court testimony, that she is not above providing false information on a job application, and her signature on any document of confidentiality is hardly worth the ink.

Nine

CAMPAIGNING AGAINST FOOD

Arguably one of the more questionable – if not downright strange – aspects of the animal rights movement is the on-going campaign against fast food restaurants and even milk. That's almost like being against nourishment.

Yet, in the animal rights world, where many of the leading activists are also the most extremist vegans, that may not be such a stretch of logic. After all, putting out of business any establishment or corporation that bases its profit on the consumption of animal products, whether beef, pork, poultry, eggs or even milk, must be a top priority.

In its effort to promote vegetarianism, PETA has declared war on McDonalds, Burger King and other chains, and the dairy and beef industries. There are many aspects of this campaign, and some of them might be considered downright disgusting by reasonable people. You be the judge.

In the fall of 2000, PETA started handing out "Milk Sucker" trading cards to school-age youngsters at several locations around the country. Patterned after baseball trading cards, these Milk Suckers featured characters called "Chubby Charlie," "Pimply Patty," "Loogie Louie" and "Windy Wanda." These four anti-milk poster children were held up as examples of what happens to people who consume dairy products: acne, flatulence and phlegm.

The campaign also advised kids that milk had been linked to far more threatening health problems, such as cancer, osteoporosis, heart disease and stroke. A deplorable offshoot of this campaign was aimed directly at former New York Mayor Rudolph Giuliani, and coincided with a television message sponsored by the Physicians Committee for Responsible Medicine, which was rejected by at least four major television outlets in New York City.

Who can blame them? The billboard advertisement sponsored by PETA included a photo of the now-legendary mayor with the familiar white milk moustache, only the message did not say "Got Milk?" like the genuine advertisements sponsored by the dairy industry.

This billboard campaign began after Giuliani announced that he had prostate cancer, upon which animal rights activists seized, because there is growing contention that milk, or perhaps calcium, or maybe a milk additive, contributes to the appearance of this disease. Apparently, the foundation for much of this anti-milk rhetoric was a Physician's Health Study, portrayed by the National Dairy Council as "a preliminary 'observational' study, which does not show a cause-and-effect relationship."

Regardless, PETA's billboard had this caption below the smiling Giuliani face: "Got prostate cancer?"

In a public attempt to justify PETA's crude attack on the mayor (whose diagnosis was one major reason he chose to drop out of a race for the United States Senate against former First Lady Hillary Rodham Clinton) Ingrid Newkirk penned an opinion piece that declared, "We knew some people wouldn't like it, but the message is more important than our discomfort at weathering a firestorm of criticism. The storm came – and with it, our message that dairy products can kill was spread far and wide."

Actually, what spread far and wide was PETA's fame, or infamy depending upon one's perspective, and the publicity generated as a result of this escapade was exactly what PETA was seeking.

Newkirk asserted that various studies have linked dairy consumption to prostate cancer. The Harvard School of Public Health was not so certain, however, noting in its own study released in April of that year that there might be a "possible" link between large-quantity dairy product consumption, but only in terms of a "modest increase" in the potential to develop prostate cancer. The Harvard study said the issue has not been settled, and suggested more study was appropriate.

Further muddying this water was a column by Dr. Gabe Mirkin in which he reported that, "A provocative study from Harvard Medical School shows that men who eat diary products regularly have a 30 percent greater chance of suffering prostate cancer than those who eat less than half a serving per day."

Countering that, and adding to the confusion, was a statement from June M. Chan, an epidemiologist at the Harvard School of Public Health: "We do not, based on this study, recommend that men drastically change their intake of dairy foods."

The April 4, 2000 issue of *USAToday* carried an Associated Press report that perhaps clarified the issue, perhaps not. That report explained that between 1982 and 1984, 20,882 male doctors had been questioned about their diet, including consumption of milk, skim milk, ice cream and cheese. Over the following ten years, the report said, 904 of these doctors developed prostate cancer. That's less than five percent.

In September of 2000, the dairy industry fought back. In public statements, the National Fluid Milk Processor Promotion Board and National Dairy Council accused PETA and PCRM of using the anti-milk campaign to bring attention to the broader animal rights cause. On Sept. 12, the Dairy Council went on the offensive, issuing a statement that read, in part: "Reputable researchers and health organizations — including the very researchers who conducted the research PCRM refers to — disagree with PCRM's position on this issue. In fact, PCRM's views have been repeatedly denounced by the American Medical Association (AMA), the National Osteoporosis Foundation (NOF), and the American Council on Science and Health (ACSH), among others."

Putting that in perspective, the author recalls being once told by a doctor during a physical examination that "All men, if they live long enough, eventually develop prostate cancer."

Attacking the Chains

When it comes to pushing a meatless diet, nobody does it better than radical animal rights activists, and PETA has led that charge with its all-out assault on McDonalds, by unleashing its "Unhappy Meal" campaign. This effort was a not-so-subtle spoof of McDonald's own highly-successful "Happy Meal" package for children. The package showed the Ronald McDonald clown image holding a blood-soaked knife, and inside were dismembered toy animals. PETA threatened to take this campaign worldwide, handing out the packages to unsuspecting children here and abroad.

PETA in 2000 complained publicly about McDonald's use of eggs and pork supplied by U.S. producers who allegedly confined their animals in stalls or cages that the animal rights group arbitrarily decided were too small.

On Aug. 23, McDonald's Corporation announced that it had adopted new standards in an attempt to address the concerns of the animal rights critics. These standards, according to a company spokesman, had been written by the company's own "panel of experts." The announcement allowed McDonalds to portray itself as a leader on the issue of reform.

Whether McDonalds caved in to pressure from PETA is open for debate, but it set the stage for PETA to mount a similar campaign against other fast food restaurant chains.

It also provided for one of the more amusing counter-attacks to come along in years. On the night of Sept. 20, vandals attacked PETA's headquarters in Norfolk, Virginia with spray paint, leaving a pair of golden arches painted on the front of the building. McDonald's long-recognized trademark are the golden arches. The vandals left one more thing: raw hamburger was thrown at the building and left on the grounds.

That certainly didn't deter PETA, which next set its sights on Jack In The Box. In a letter to the company that arrived Dec. 1, 2000, PETA threatened the same kind of negative campaign against the San Diego, California-based fast food corporation that had been mounted against McDonalds.

The next headline PETA garnered in its battle against fast-food chains came in January 2001, when the organization opened yet another campaign, this one against the Burger King chain. PETA announced in a Jan. 9 press release that it would, the next day, start a "negative publicity campaign" against Burger King in an effort to force it to follow the McDonalds example.

The campaign was vicious with PETA producing a poster depicting the familiar Burger King motif with the logo "Murder King."

Likewise, PETA pounced on Wendy's using a facsimile of that chain's motif but substituting the name "Wretch's Old Fashioned Murderers" and using a "Wicked Wendy" character holding a bloody knife.

Meanwhile, and perhaps not surprisingly to those who

believe there is more than a casual connection between the two groups, PETA's campaign against McDonalds brought out the ALF, which had an already established history of attacking fast food restaurants. These attacks, and many other incidents, have been summarized by the National Animal Interest Alliance on the Internet.

The earliest attacks listed by NAIA start with a Jan. 4, 1997 strike against franchises for McDonalds, Arby's and Kentucky Fried Chicken in Salt Lake City, Utah that were among 20 stores vandalized by shots fired through their store windows. Nobody claimed credit for the vandalism.

However, six weeks later, ALF did take credit for an attack on a McDonalds in Troy, Michigan on Feb. 15.

Two months later, on April 19, unidentified animal rights activists smashed windows and otherwise vandalized the Golden Coral Restaurant in Maryland.

On Aug. 12, 1999, the campaign against McDonalds went international, when suspected ALF terrorists, leaving the telltale "ALF" letters spray painted at the site, hit a McDonalds in Antwerp, Belgium, burning it to the ground.

Back in the United States, ALF trashed four different McDonald's restaurants in Nassau on New York's Long Island the night of Oct. 16, 1999 breaking windows and leaving spray painted graffiti.

Sometime during the night of April 8, 2000, two Arby's outlets, a Burger King restaurant and a leather shop were again vandalized in Salt Lake City, Utah. The culprits left the "ALF" initials spray painted on the walls.

A Burger King located on the University of Buffalo, New York was raided the night of Feb. 5, 2001 by ALF vandals who smashed windows and a glass door, and spray-painted the walls. Two nights later, on Feb. 7, a McDonald's restaurant in Washington D.C. was vandalized and the damage was attributed to ALF.

On March 29, two animal rights activists identified as Sarah Ann Clifton and Nicholas J. Patch – apparently not officially affiliated with any group as they were not so identified in press reports – were arrested after they entered a Burger King restaurant in Maryland and jumped on the counter in an apparent attempt to close the establishment. They were charged with unlawful entry.

On June 5, the anti-Burger King campaign opened in Dayton, Ohio. There, students from the Wilbur Wright Middle School were confronted by animal rights activists identifying themselves as members of "Mercy for Animals." The demonstrators gave the youngsters paper crowns reminiscent of the Burger King prop, but these had tiny pigs and cows impaled on the points.

Burger King reached an agreement with PETA in June 2001, promising to exceed the conditions to which McDonald's had acceded.

The campaign against Wendy's did not go so well for PETA, because the restaurant chain simply responded that it had already adopted practices that exceeded what the other chains were doing. Wendy's issued an Animal Welfare Program Fact Sheet that explained its position. PETA's Friedrich responded with a lengthy press release criticizing the fact sheet, essentially holding Wendy's responsible for all kinds of alleged problems that seemed to be more of an issue at the meat supply level than anything Wendy's, as a corporation, could address.

In September, animal rights activists attacked the McDonalds outlet in Tucson, Arizona. On the night of Sept. 8, they hit a restaurant leaving ALF and ELF initials spray painted on the walls, along with assorted vulgarities, before causing heavy damage to the structure with a firebomb. Two weeks later, on Sept. 20, they were at it again, this time defacing the Ronald McDonald statue in front of the Ronald

McDonald House, which hosts families of children who are being treated for serious illnesses in a local hospital. In addition to the ALF and ELF initials and vulgarities, someone spray painted a swastika on the statue.

Perhaps underscoring the seriousness of ALF's intentions against McDonalds – and any other franchises – on its Internet website, ALF listed a full page of "tips" on how to attack such a restaurant "legally" by engaging in offensive behavior.

It strikes some people as more than a mere coincidence that PETA's overt campaigns, whether they are against fur stores, fast food chains or meat producers, seem frequently to coincide with covert operations mounted against the same targets by ALF, and vice versa. How does one explain the all-too-frequently-coincidental PETA campaigns and ALF attacks?

From Eggs to Steak

There is no coincidence between PETA campaigns and ALF attacks, in the opinion of Tom DeWeese, president of the American Policy Center, a privately funded, nonprofit, 501 (c) (4), tax-exempt grassroots action and education foundation dedicated to the promotion of free enterprise and limited government regulations over commerce and individuals.

In an Oct. 25, 2001 essay, DeWeese made it abundantly clear that he believes the two organizations are directly linked, declaring: "ALF can be described as nothing short of the terrorist arm of PETA."

Is it mere coincidence that PETA has carried on a long campaign against the use of fur in clothing, and ALF or "unidentified persons" conduct raids on mink farms across the country?

Would there be any connection between PETA's campaign against meat and the Mother's Day 1999 arson at Childer's Meat Company in Eugene, Oregon for which ALF claimed credit?

Is there any correlation between PETA's support of the 1999 Primate Freedom Tour and the June 25, 1999 firebombing of a truck belonging to Worldwide Primates, Inc. in Miami, Florida for which ALF took responsibility? A group called Action for Animals (AF) sponsored the Primate Freedom Tour, and on its website, the group acknowledges that PETA supplied several thousand dollars in financial support of AFA activities in 2000.

How does one explain the timing of a boycott effort against Neiman Marcus mounted by PETA, a fur protest held at the San Francisco store on Feb. 28, 2000 and, the night before that protest, an ALF raid on the building that left 29 windows smashed and an estimated $100,000 in property damage?

Over the course of several years, ALF has, by its own admission, done things that PETA has – in public, anyway – only talked about, and in terms usually vague enough to allow the actions to be disavowed on one level, but somewhat condoned on other levels. The crimes have not been limited to mink farmers or beef producers, as in the case of an attempted arson at San Francisco's Fulton Poultry Processors the night of Dec. 20, 1999. Four "incendiary devices" were planted but only one actually went off.

On May 16, 2000, ALF claimed responsibility for raiding an egg farm in Burlington, Washington. They stole 200 chickens.

On July 2, 2000, ALF left its initials painted on a concrete wall at the Rose Acre chicken farm near North Vernon, Indiana. They burned a truck and caused an estimated $100,000 in damage.

In January 2001, the Philadelphia, Pennsylvania-based Pride of the Sea fish distributorship was struck twice by ALF, first on the 5th and again on the 27th, with damage primarily limited to slashed truck tires.

Yet, it is beef producers that have endured the bulk of ALF attacks. After being hit twice by the ALF, Jersey Cuts in Howell, New Jersey called it quits in July 1999. The second attack was a firebombing that destroyed three trucks at the cost of $180,000.

ALF claimed credit for a Dec. 11, 2000 arson that destroyed a truck at the Ferry Market beef distribution warehouse in Vancouver, British Columbia. Two weeks later, ALF delivered a Christmas "present" of sorts when it put seven firebombs under as many trucks at a meat distributorship in Burnaby, B.C.

Firebombs placed under two trucks at the Schaller and Weber meat packing plant in Long Island City, New York on March 2, 2001. An ALF communiqué claimed that the arson was done in support of two "activists" who had been involved in property crimes.

Near Eindhoven, The Netherlands on March 25, 2001, ALF took credit for a slaughterhouse arson that caused $4 million in damages.

Quite possibly the most interesting reaction to the animal rights fanaticism that produced the arsons might fall into the realm of "conspiracy theory." On Friday, March 2, 2001, Paul Gilfeather, Whitehall editor for the *London Mirror*, disclosed that investigators with Britain's Ministry of Agriculture had been "probing the idea" that animal rights extremists might have been responsible for the outbreak and spread of the foot and mouth outbreak in English cattle herds. In his column, Gilfeather suggested that British agriculture officials theorized that the world could be facing a "Blofeld Threat." It was an allusion to the fictional arch-criminal Ernst Stavro Blofeld from the James Bond novels by the late Ian Fleming. Blofeld was a fiend who, in *On Her Majesty's Secret Service*, plotted to unleash the disease all over the globe.

Gilfeather wrote, "Many people in the Ministry think it is no coincidence that farming has suffered swine fever and foot-and-mouth outbreaks within nine months after years and years of healthy herds."

The idea was repeated by American writer John Fulton Lewis in an April 10, 2001 column for Alliance For America. Lewis detailed Gilfeather's allegations, then expanded upon it, noting, "For nearly two years Scotland Yard, America's FBI and Central Intelligence Agency and the international police security network, Interpol, have all been alert to the possibility that the purposeful spread of diseases harmful to agriculture or human beings is a possible threat. Such is known to be in the arsenal of terrorist mastermind Osama bin Laden. The FBI, in listing ELF…as the prime eco-terrorist organization, has indicated it would not be surprised if the use of toxic or contaminating substances were attempted by some domestic elements engaged in anarchy or animal rights extremism."

That was written five months almost to the day before the terrorist attacks on New York and the Pentagon.

However, one would be hard pressed to show any kind of link between animal rights radicals and Middle Eastern fanatics, other than comparing one to the other for their equally extremist philosophies.

Yet, it is disturbing that both PETA's Newkirk and Friedrich had suggested that an outbreak of foot-and-mouth disease among domestic livestock would be "good" for America. Both said that such an outbreak would force more people to become vegetarians, and Friedrich said dying from the disease would save the animals from being taken to a slaughterhouse.

What's the difference between releasing a deadly disease to force people to become vegetarians, and unleashing terrorism in an irrational effort to make the entire world bow to the radical Islamic agenda?

Vegetable Matters

PETA and even ALF may want to take issue with another group of environmental extremists, the ones who have a small, but rather curious history of destroying vegetable and crop research. For those activists promoting a vegetarian diet, this particular crop of radicals might pose as great a threat as vegans do to meat eaters.

In August 1999, radicals operating under the banner of "Seeds of Resistance," a group about which next to nothing is known. Whoever they are, this bunch claimed responsibility for an attack on a plot of experimental corn being grown at the University of Maine's Rogers Farm. Ironically, the experiment under way had to do with plant gene splicing in an effort to create plants that are more resistant to diseases, thus less in need of herbicide reinforcement. Herbicides are the bane of many environmentalists.

On Jan. 11, 2000, a group claiming the title "Reclaim the Seeds" raided the U.S. Department of Agriculture's Agricultural Research Service's Western Regional Research Center at the University of California, in Albany, California near San Francisco. They destroyed experimental plants.

Four months later, on April 8, another anti-agriculture raid was staged by a self-proclaimed "anti-biotech" group calling itself the "Petaluma Pruners." Their target was grape plant root stock being developed by the Vinifera Corporation.

In Hawaii, a May 9, 2000 raid on the island of Kauai

destroyed an experimental corn crop at the Novartis center. This sabotage was the work of a group calling itself the "Menehune."

On July 31, 2000 near the tiny town of Dusty, Washington, unidentified anti-biotech saboteurs raided a five-acre plot of genetically engineered canola being developed by Monsanto. Canola seeds are used to produce canola oil, considered a very healthy cooking oil that helps lower blood cholesterol.

An attack on the Siminis research center in Filer, Idaho about six miles west of Twin Falls on June 10, 2001 resulted in destruction of experimental pea patches and removal of plants from several of the patches.

There does not appear to be even the slightest connection between the anti-biotechnology extremists and animal rights radicals – and certainly not PETA – other than dedication to a cause, or just the need to destroy other people's property to push their own individual agenda, whatever that may be.

Ten

MARCH 4 – MAY 1, 2002

Racketeering is a term normally associated with rather large, muscular and dangerous people who scowl a lot, have colorful nicknames and pasta diets, long black cars, loaded guns within easy reach, and knowledge of the locations of shallow graves in remote wooded areas of New Jersey or Upstate New York. At least, that's the Hollywood stereotype.

In real life, the term "racketeering" can cover a broad range of activities, some of them surprising to the average citizen. Believe it or not, people involved in organized protests over various issues (abortion, gun control, you name it) could be committing acts that fall within the scope of federal racketeering statutes, as noted in Chapter Eight. What is required is that these individuals conduct their activities in ways that harass, intimidate, and perhaps endanger the people against whom or whose activities they are protesting; things that go beyond acts or speech constitutionally protected by the First Amendment.

Anti-hunters, for example, have been known to destroy property, set booby traps, verbally harass hunters and wildlife, and on a couple of occasions throw themselves in front of hunters' gun muzzles. They have planned to do these things, which, depending upon the view of an investigator or prosecutor, might constitute a conspiracy.

But a court case that got the attention of animal rights extremists because it had the potential to put them in jeopardy of being arrested and sent to jail or cost them millions of dollars had nothing at all to do with animal rights.

In mid-April 2002, the United States Supreme Court agreed to hear the appeal of several anti-abortion activists against whom lower courts had issued judgments involving multi-millions of dollars in favor of the National Organization for Women (NOW). Seeking protection from abortion foes, who had established histories of organizing or participating in demonstrations and harassment of abortion clinic staffers and clients at various locations around the country, NOW singled out some of these people and went after them in court.

In addition to seeking judgments against protesters and provocateurs, NOW's case also focused on individuals who may have approved of acts of violence against abortion clinics and people who operated them, while not actually engaging in any of those actions personally.

Significant about this case was the fact that NOW had filed its original complaints under the Racketeer Influenced and Corrupt Organizations (RICO) Act, a piece of federal legislation more commonly associated with nailing Mafia dons than silencing pro-life protesters. But this is no ordinary complaint, in that NOW had brought its original action as a civil lawsuit under a section of the RICO Act that allows civil complaints.

All of this was detailed in an April 22, 2002 internet column at AnimalRights.net by PETA critic Brian Carnell, who noted that this case, while hardly related directly to animal rights, certainly posed a direct threat to the tactics of animal rights extremists.

If RICO can stop anti-abortion zealots, it could be used as a hammer against animal rights activists in ways they could not have imagined years ago.

People for the Ethical Treatment of Animals had this

one figured out quickly because, according to the Associated Press, PETA was one of the organizations that had encouraged the high court to hear the case. Still fresh in PETA's memory was the RICO lawsuit it had settled with Huntingdon Laboratories in December 1997, which included dropping of charges against Ingrid Newkirk and undercover operative Michelle Rokke.

While there are certainly First Amendment issues involved in PETA activities, it would be fair to observe that PETA's interest in the NOW case has very little to do with an interest in judicial activism.

PETA clearly would not want its own activities to be subject to RICO statutes, because the organization was already under the scrutiny of a Congressional House subcommittee for its questionable links to the Animal Liberation Front and Earth Liberation Front. Besides, Newkirk, Rokke and another PETA staffer, Mary Beth Sweetland, had only barely skated away from RICO charges in the Huntingdon settlement. Would they want to face the possibility of such charges in the future?

There is more, and it brings a new perspective into the fight by dairy farmers, mink ranchers, laboratories, circuses and hunters against animal rights extremists. Instead of going after PETA and other animal rights organizations on purely philosophical grounds, bringing RICO accusations into the debate could put such extremist groups into a different peril altogether. Ironically, opponents of animal rights extremism note that the RICO issue might open an opportunity to seriously cripple such groups by somewhat the same means that federal agents have nailed mobsters, not with guns but with ledgers. Recall that Chicago mob boss Al Capone tumbled to tax laws, not bullets.

In PETA's particular case, the problem is not concealment of taxable revenue, but in the organization's tax-exempt status. After years of offering what critics felt had been direct aid to animal rights terrorist groups and individuals, and encouraging the kind of conduct that leads to criminal acts, PETA found itself challenged by a complaint to the Internal Revenue Service from a private group asking that PETA's tax exemption be revoked.

Enter the Center

On March 2, 2002 the Center for the Defense of Free Enterprise (CDFE) filed a formal complaint with IRS Commissioner Charles O. Rossotti, seeking to have PETA's 501(c)(3) status revoked.

CDFE is a non-partisan group based in Bellevue, Washington and, to the environmental and animal rights movements, it is probably the closest thing imaginable to their incarnation of the anti-Christ. Founded by Alan Gottlieb and author Ron Arnold, the CDFE is a rather Spartan operation compared to typical foundations, functioning on a shoestring budget. However, one must recall what a handful of Spartans did at the Battle of Thermopylae.

Gottlieb and Arnold have no great compassion for environmental extremism or animal rights zealotry. Gottlieb is a renowned fund raiser for conservative causes and has a degree in nuclear engineering from the University of Tennessee. Perhaps better known for his work on Second Amendment issues, Gottlieb is also author of several books and is frequently published in newspapers around the country.

Arnold is CDFE's executive vice president, and a former member of the Sierra Club. The author of several books, including *EcoTerror* and (with Gottlieb) *Trashing the Economy* (which devotes a section to PETA as an organization that is trashing the economy and killing jobs) he is an advocate of the Wise Use Movement, and has appeared on various national news programs. He is also a media consultant, operating his own firm in Bellevue.

Arnold and Gottlieb have spent more than a decade tracking PETA activities and their association with ALF and ELF. They are convinced the organizations are directly, and improperly, linked.

This was not the first time that CDFE had gone to the IRS with a complaint about the activities of a specific group. Barely two weeks before, on Feb. 17, CDFE had made a similar request to Rossotti to revoke the tax-exempt status of the Environmental Working Group, a Washington, D.C.-based environmental organization that Arnold contended was actually a lobbying group.

EWG had, Arnold complained, "functioned as an illegal political action organization" that had taken a $1.6 million grant from the liberal Joyce Foundation to lobby the 2002 Farm Bill. He also asserted that EWG had lobbied for a year in California without registering as a lobbying organization, and that EWG concealed its California lobbying expenditures while operating as a project of another liberal entity, the Tides Foundation in San Francisco.

In its 12-page complaint to the IRS about the animal rights organization, the CDFE detailed its case against PETA's tax-exempt status, noting the group's history of support for ALF activities, its financial contributions to Coronado and others, and statements made by Newkirk and other PETA associates that advocate arson and other types of property destruction.

Gottlieb indicated to a reporter for the *Washington Times* March 5 that the CDFE's action could startle American taxpayers who may not have realized PETA's tax-exempt status. He further suggested that many people might quickly conclude that their taxes had been "subsidizing PETA's activities" because animal rights supporters could deduct their donations as "charitable contributions" on their income tax returns.

After detailing PETA's curious history, Arnold publicly wondered why neither the IRS nor Congress had looked into PETA's activities. He did not have long to wait for a Congressional response, because two days after the CDFE complaint was filed, Colorado's Rep. Scott McInnis sent his letter, detailed in Chapter Four, to PETA's Newkirk seeking answers to the very questions to which Arnold was alluding.

Newkirk and PETA attorney Jeffrey Kerr were quick to respond. Newkirk called the CDFE complaint a "straw man."

"They're trying to create dirt where no dirt exists," she insisted.

Kerr was even more terse, calling it "a smear campaign."

Smear or not, the announcement was enough to put CDFE on the evening news programs, especially on the Fox News Network, and on the pages of daily newspapers across the country.

Equally significant to the CDFE complaint was PETA's response. It was rather muted, and for an organization known to be litigious for even the most seemingly minor affronts, this legal howitzer shot across PETA's bow did not find the organization's attorneys trooping into the nearest court with a lawsuit.

Perhaps that is because Kerr was too busy writing his 12-page response to McInnis, while PETA was issuing statements to the Associated Press, published March 16, that labeled McInnis' questioning "new McCarthyism."

In rebuttal to that allegation, Josh Penry, a McInnis staffer, perhaps clarified the issue better than anyone: "The remarkable thing is these people seem surprised that they're getting called on the carpet for giving money to an eco-terrorist group. Here's a hint: Stop underwriting domestic terrorist groups and people will leave you alone."

Complaint Amended

The issue may have rested there for IRS to do its work, but Arnold pressed his cause, amending his original complaint on May 1 with a follow-up letter to Rossotti in which Arnold called attention to "irregularities" in PETA's reporting of grants and allocations. These were, Arnold explained to this author, pretty interesting "irregularities."

PETA had failed to provide schedules of its grants and allocations to other organizations for two consecutive years when it filed its IRS Form 990 reports for the fiscal years ending July 31, 1997 and July 31, 1998. Arnold estimated that the PETA Form 990 reports on file with the IRS contained "no detailed accounting for nearly one million dollars of PETA funds..."

In his second letter to Rossotti, Arnold contended that omission of this information on two annual PETA reports "is a matter of public concern," because the public has a legitimate right to know whether the organization may have been providing financial support of any kind to any organization that might be considered a domestic terrorist group by the FBI.

Arnold may have a point, because PETA's Form 990 for the 1999 fiscal year (ending July 31, 2000) does include an attachment stretching 11 pages that details PETA's grants and allocations for that period.

What is listed in that document? Among other things, two allocations for $300,000 and $700,000, respectively, to the Foundation to Support Animal Protection are identified.

There are two more payments, one for $50,000 and the other for $200,000 to the Institute for In Vitro Sciences, which works on reducing the use of animals in research and testing. Other donors to IIVS include Colgate-Palmolive, Gillette, Johnson & Johnson, Kimberly-Clark, Mattel, and Proctor & Gamble.

Over the course of several months, monthly payments of $500 went to Helga Tacreiter, perhaps best known for designing "pasture pillows" that resemble cows. Tacreiter makes three sizes of "Cowches," ranging in price from $300 to $800. She has operated a farm in New Jersey where cows are given shelter of sorts, allegedly so they don't wind up in a butcher shop.

Two payments of $500 each went to the Illinois Humane Political Action Committee on April 26 and May 24, 2000 but according to the report, six grants of $500 each went to the Illinois HPAC on March 3. Vastly exceeding that, "various" payments apparently totaling $130,348.36 went to PETA Europe and another $105,763.86 was allocated to Stiching PETA Netherlands, and $215,305.69 for PETA Deutschland in Germany.

Go down through the list and you will find grants and allocations ranging upwards from $25, to all kinds of groups and individuals.

There is only one consistency. Each allocation is identified as a contribution "to support their program activities." This is the same nebulous purpose for which the $1,500 grant went to ELF's Craig Rosebraugh.

One wonders, for example, what the "program activities" of Animal Liberation in Australia might entail that it received $2,000 from PETA in March 2000.

Elsewhere on the Form 990, you will find that during FY 1999, PETA reported that it spent over $1.3 million on consultants, slightly over $2 million on media and press support, and just over $796,000 on legal fees. They also spent over $2.6 million on postage and shipping, including $707,264 on fund raising.

Despite PETA's report that its total revenue, even during FY 1999, was over $15.8 million and its expenses were listed at over $17.6 million, there is still a great deal of money at stake, and you can bet that PETA would not be happy to lose its tax-exempt status.

Newkirk acknowledged that fact in the March 5, 2002 edition of the *Washington Times*, telling a reporter that losing that tax-exempt status would devastate PETA. The newspaper said more than $13 million was donated to the organization during the tax year that ended July 31, 2001.

"Anytime an organization loses its tax-exempt status, there are some donors who will give less or not at all," Newkirk conceded to the newspaper.

Newkirk subsequently defended PETA as "squeaky clean" in the March 9 edition of the *Washington Times*, and even suggested to reporters that the CDFE action could backfire politically by causing typical donors to contribute more money than usual.

Timing Everything

They say that timing is everything, and in the broad scheme of things, the timing of one Bryan Pease could not have been more unfortunate for anyone paying attention to the problems PETA was experiencing during the first few months of 2002.

And just who is Bryan Pease? He is the University at Buffalo second-year Law School student who has more than one claim to fame. He is the son of a prominent federal attorney, and he is also an animal rights activist who has been arrested for his activities more than once.

The co-president of Cornell Students for the Ethical Treatment of Animals (also identified as Cornell Coalition for Animal Defense), Pease was arrested by police for trespassing on the Marshall Farms USA property near North Rose, NY on Feb. 21, 2002 at 1:15 a.m. He was attired in full camouflage when this encounter occurred, and police were rightly suspicious because on the night of Dec. 5, 2001, Marshall Farms was burglarized and 25 beagle hounds were taken.

ALF took credit for that caper and promised there would be a return engagement. Whether Pease could be called an ALF member or sympathizer might be determined by one's definition of what that would be, flavored with some knowledge of Pease's history.

Pease evidently gets around, because the Feb. 21 incident was just over a month after he had been arrested – on Jan. 15 – in Conway, Arkansas and charged with commercial burglary, third degree battery, criminal mischief, resisting arrest and fleeing arrest. He was among some 30 demonstrators staging an event in front of Stephens, Inc., a banking firm that has provided some financial support to Huntingdon Life Sciences in England, the facility that had been targeted by animal rights extremists.

This time, Pease was in the company of people claiming to be members of Stop Huntingdon Animal Cruelty (SHAC), discussed briefly in Chapter Four.

In an Op-Ed piece published by the *New York Post* on March 15, writer Steven Milloy of the Cato Institute identified Pease as "an ALF sympathizer at least." Milloy also noted that Pease, while a student at Cornell, "promoted a speech by an Animal Defense League member on the 'historical uses of violence in liberation movements'." He also said that Pease had been a supporter of convicted cop-killer Mumia Abu-Jamal, who brutally shot to death Philadelphia police officer Daniel Faulkner on Dec. 9, 1981. Abu-Jamal has since become something of a folk hero to the far left anti-establishment fringe.

For anyone paying attention to the headlines, they might have spotted stories about Pease and his links to ALF at the very moment Congress was asking those embarrassing questions about the PETA-ALF connection, and the IRS had just received CDFE's request to cancel PETA's tax exempt status. Probably not the best time to have some sort of ALF-related terrorist activity hitting the news columns.

One should give credit to ALF for at least allowing some time for political dust to settle before taking credit for yet another outrage, this time the May 15 firebombing of a poultry plant in Indiana. As ALF raids go, this one was pretty much a bust, because it only managed to destroy a single truck. Perhaps the most significant accomplishment of the raid was that it kept ALF in the headlines.

Expert Observations

It did not take long for the press to move beyond the news releases and public statements by CDFE's Arnold and PETA's Newkirk.

Arguably, two of the more reliable authorities on PETA are found at the American University College of Law in Washington, D.C.

Interviewed by the *Spokane Spokesman-Review* (March 5, 2002) John Lawley, a student at the university who had conducted research on PETA's tax exemption, suggested that CDFE might be on thin ice if it were only complaining about PETA's contribution to the defense fund of ELF's Craig Rosebraugh.

In an interview with the author, Lawley said that the Rosebraugh donation, alone, probably would not be sufficient to cause the IRS to revoke PETA's tax-exempt status. Quite likely, he added, even the contributions to the Coronado and Troen defenses might not have that much weight, because there is apparently no provision in the tax code to prevent a tax-exempt organization from contributing money to a legal defense fund.

Wrote Lawley: "This author believes…that an inquiry into the potential grounds for revocation on the basis of the PETA's financial transactions reveals that such a basis is at best weak."

Lawley had written in his study that "Eco-Terrorism clearly violates public policy." To what degree PETA's connections with ALF and ELF may affect its status would have to be determined by the IRS or in a court of law, he acknowledged.

On a strictly non-legal level, Lawley conceded that it does PETA no good at all in the public relations arena to be giving money to organizations or underground groups, or individuals, that take credit for arson, burglary and property destruction, much less $1,500 to help a member of such an organization with his legal defense.

Lawley's opinion may hardly be enough to keep PETA's status out of jeopardy, however. Indeed, a professor of law at the same university had a considerably different perspective.

Professor Kenneth Anderson, who teaches non-profit tax law at the university, and who was the legal editor for *Crimes of War: What the Public Needs to Know* did not share Lawley's opinion about the lack of PETA's potential liabilities. His observation: "Anything PETA does with money has to be a charitable purpose. How can it be a charitable purpose if they're giving it to a terrorist organization?"

Anderson – in the interview with the Spokane newspaper – alluded to a point made earlier in this chapter about how PETA, in its tax return, identified each of its contributions, no matter who the recipient, as being for the purpose of supporting "program activities." This is far too vague, in Anderson's opinion, to suit the IRS. Anderson explained that in the eyes of the IRS, it could constitute improper record keeping, an assessment made all the more plausible by the string of changing explanations PETA put forth about the Rosebraugh donation when it was first revealed.

Clearly, PETA could not get its story straight about where that money went and whether PETA knew what it was specifically for until – backed into a corner – the organization had no other alternative than to provide full disclosure. One might reasonably ask PETA why, from the outset, it did not simply explain where the money went? Was PETA trying to conceal something it knew could be potentially embarrassing?

The professor explained to the newspaper that records must be properly maintained for any organization to retain its tax-exempt status. He noted, however, that it would not be likely PETA could lose its status over one such questionable donation, and it would hardly be an offense that resulted in a jail sentence for anyone.

But to lose the tax-exempt status would be a severe setback for PETA because its contributors could no longer declare those donations on their IRS forms for a tax deduction. As a result, they may be less likely to contribute, turning elsewhere to make charitable donations for their own tax purposes.

Why would a newspaper in Spokane, Washington be interested in an IRS complaint against an animal rights group based in Virginia? There are several good reasons. Washington State University at Pullman – scene of an ALF attack in August 1991 – is south of Spokane. CDFE's headquarters is located in another Washington city, Bellevue. Spokane is in Eastern Washington, which is a hub of cattle ranching, hunting, fishing, agriculture and both livestock and agricultural research

But most important of all, U.S. Congressman George Nethercutt, who represents Washington's 5th Congressional district in which Spokane is centrally located, is no fan of the animal rights movement or the domestic terrorism it has spawned. He has proposed legislation that would stiffen fines and penalties for eco-terrorists or anyone who supports their activities.

Of particular interest, Nethercutt's legislation would not only enhance penalties, but also allow the FBI to investigate such eco-terror crimes under the RICO Act.

Eleven

THE ENEMIES WITHIN

Philosophical differences are to be expected in any movement, whether social or political, and these differences intensify when the focus is on an issue certain to attract and arouse anyone with an activist bent.

No doubt many in the animal rights movement sincerely abhor the use of violence and criminal wrongdoing while others publicly insist they do not endorse it but hypocritically give it a condoning wink. Still others are bomb-setting extremists who are in every sense terrorists as much as the IRA or Hezbollah or al Qaeda. There are, within the animal rights community, differences of opinion about direction and emphasis; should the movement be based upon the principle of pure "animal rights" or should it concentrate more on "animal welfare." One is not the other.

As author Kathleen Marquardt noted in her 1993 book *AnimalScam*, "PETA is an animal 'rights' or animal 'liberation' group. It bears no similarity to 'humane' or 'animal welfare' organizations with which PETA likes to be confused. Animal welfare organizations seek the humane treatment of animals. Animal rights groups, in contrast, believe that humane treatment is irrelevant: all use of animals by people, no matter how humane or necessary, should be banned."

Marquardt put it bluntly: "Animal rights is a disaster not just for humanity, but for animals as well. It rejects the concept of anim ı welfare. That means no wildlife management, veterinary medicine, or captive breeding of endangered species. It means needless suffering and death for both people and animals, and even the extinction of some species. Animal rights is not out to improve animal care, but to abolish it."

One-time PETA general counsel Gary Francione might agree, perhaps not intentionally. A professor of law at Rutgers University and director of the Rutgers Animal Rights Law Center, Francione is co-author of a pamphlet entitled *Demonstrating and Civil Disobedience: A Legal Guide for Activists.* Certainly one of the more legally knowledgeable leaders of the animal rights movement, Francione clerked for Supreme Court Justice Sandra Day O'Connor in 1982-83. He practiced law in New York and was a member of the University of Pennsylvania Law School faculty.

By his own admission, writing in *The Animals' Voice* (Vol. 4, No. 2), Francione noted, "The theory of animal rights simply is not consistent with the theory of animal welfare." Francione is a devoted advocate of animal rights, and apparently not a proponent of animal welfare.

The philosophical division within the animal rights community may explain why some people demonstrate in public while others sneak around under cover of darkness with firebombs and gas cans, spray paint and wire cutters.

It also explains why veterinarians, pet stores and animal trainers are sometimes targeted for harassment by the more extremist elements in the animal rights movement. It is almost as though the animal "rights" zealots were as much in disagreement with animal "welfare" practitioners as they are at war with everyone else, from researchers to hunters to restaurateurs to anybody who barbecues a hamburger.

Fire Starters

Some years ago, actor Charlton Heston – who was also active in politics and later was elected president of the National Rifle Association – became righteously indignant as a stockholder in Time-Warner when that company marketed obscenity-laced recordings by a rapper named Ice-T that, among other things, advocated murder of police officers.

In particular, Heston was furious over the lyrics of a recording called "Cop Killer." He attended a stockholders meeting and read the lyrics to a stunned audience, then quoted Ice-T's lyricized fantasy about sodomizing the two nieces of Al and Tipper Gore, and afterward strolled outside to meet waiting reporters, repeating the lyrics. When Heston – who related the incident to this author some years later during an interview – told the press what was in the recording, reporters told him flatly that they could not print the lyrics in their newspapers. Heston's retort: "I know, but Time/Warner is selling it!"

Heston is an incredibly effective public speaker, even in his late 70s. At the Time/Warner event, he was devastating, and it was not long afterward that the giant media conglomerate put considerable distance between itself and the rap star.

In the "Post Sept. 11" social environment, there is a legitimate question that could be posed to PETA by its supporters, based on its heavy financial support for ALF terrorists and that single $1,500 contribution to ELF's Craig Rosebraugh, about which a great deal has been made in Congress and on the Internet.

One can legitimately demand to know why PETA would have anything remotely to do with an organization that uses its website to distribute a pamphlet entitled *Starting Fires With Electrical Timers – An Earth Liberation Front Guide.*

143

Within the pages of this document are recipes for fire-bombs, designed for use by "all nonprofit groups working for animal liberation and their supporters."

The opening page contains this threat: "All other corporations, companies, businesses, institutes, colleges and think tanks are forbidden from copying this publication in part or whole. All government agencies and employees of the government are expressly forbidden from copying this publication in part or whole. Violators will be subject to prosecution or *retribution*. You have been warned."

Translation: "Do to us what Heston did to Time/Warner by exposing the content of our 'product,' and we will get even."

This 37-page document includes "The Four Rules of Arson," offers advice on where to place incendiary devices, the construction of electrical timers, tips on making devices with kitchen timers or digital timers, fuel requirements for buildings and even igniting a firebomb with a light bulb igniter.

Wrapping up this arsonists directory are tips on how to avoid getting caught, such as advice to purchase bomb components "well in advance of any action" and "far from where you live and far from the target." The reason: "…it would be easy for investigators to visit each store in the area to review video surveillance tapes and interview cashiers." Terrorists are also advised against purchasing all of their components at the same place, cautioned against using certain types of tape because DNA might be recovered from its sticky surface, and warned about working with certain timers and devices that could detonate in their hands.

ELF's guide is not simply the handiwork of some overly imaginative high school science student or a youngster with his first chemistry set. This pamphlet contains explicit directions, and was written for people intent on creating havoc.

Here's a telling passage about the mindset of those responsible for producing this document: "Guarantee destruction of the target through careful planning and execution. Take no shortcuts. Do thorough reconnaissance to eliminate surprises. Make contingency plans for anything that could go wrong. Do extensive testing of timers and igniters. Use multiple incendiary devices with generous amounts of accelerant. Never be satisfied with *possible* destruction or *probable* destruction. The objective of every action should be *assured destruction*. The risks are too high for anything else."

For the record, PETA is not promoting this document, but it has been PETA that has turned a blind, nay, winking, eye toward the group that is and the people who have used the information. PETA's Newkirk, while certainly not Time/ Warner, is no less guilty of being disingenuous about such material than Time/Warner executives had been about turning a deaf ear to the lyrics of a violent rap recording their company had been marketing.

Naturally, PETA and its supporters will insist that Newkirk has every right to speak about tearing down institutions to which she objects, and there is some Constitutional merit on that argument. But even the First Amendment has its limits. You may not yell "Fire" in a crowded theater, nor may you set one in a laboratory, barn or processing plant to destroy public or private property.

For some PETA supporters, it may be that they simply have not gotten the message or made the connection between vaguely advocating certain acts and the actual commission of those acts. Marquardt, again writing in *AnimalScam*, declared, "Publicly, animal rights leaders disguise their agenda, distracting misguided animal lovers from the movement's true goals with a continual barrage of sensational (and generally fraudulent) allegations of animal abuse...(T)he animal rights movement is built on deceit and misrepresentation. It cannot be stated strongly enough: Every time animal rights leaders open their mouths, they lie."

If "a rat is a pig is a dog is a boy," what would Newkirk call a person who merely mouths support for the work of arsonists and vandals? If she disdains violence, can you – based on Marquardt's allegation and her own remarks over the years – believe her?

To believe Newkirk, one would have to accept that she has refuted her own organization. In a statement issued after ALF claimed credit for a $500,000 arson fire at Northwest Farm Foods Co-op in June 1991, PETA said, "We cannot condemn the Animal Liberation Front…they act courageously, risking their freedom and their careers to stop the terror inflicted every day on animals in labs. (Their activities) comprise an important part of today's animal protection movement."

Harassment and Assault

In March 2000, Newkirk, accompanied by Chrissy Hynde, lead singer for the rock group the Pretenders, plus Paul Haje and Paul Chetirkin were arrested and charged with criminal mischief and trespassing in New York. The charge followed their deliberate destruction of leather garments at a Manhattan Gap store.

"Criminal mischief?" That makes it sound like some kids' prank, on the level of spreading toilet paper around a rival college frat house.

Much like the Las Vegas episode involving PETA's Dawn Carr, who hit Miss Rodeo America Brandy DeJongh in the face with a pie, or PETA's two-year stalking campaign against country singer Kenny Rogers by a person dressed as a celery stalk, the level of the criminal charge makes PETA seem like just a playful bunch of adults. The "stalk" followed Rogers on tour, holding a sign that read "Kenny Kills Chickens" because of his affiliation with a restaurant chain called Kenny Rogers' Roasters. Seems like nothing more than childish hazing, doesn't it?

The public does not often connect the animal rights movement to serious physical harm. It is a false impression, and even though physical assaults are never officially sanctioned by PETA, one does not see Newkirk or any of her colleagues rushing to a microphone to denounce a physical assault.

There was, of course, the serious beating of Huntingdon Life Sciences manager Brian Cass in February 2001 – discussed in Chapter Four – for which one of the attackers was sent to prison. Cass is not the only person to have felt the physical wrath of animal rights extremists.

Michael Skupin, one of the contestants on the program *Survivor*, was publicly demonized by PETA for having killed a pig and smearing its blood on his face during one very questionable segment of that "reality" program. Skupin, who later left the program due to injuries he suffered when he fell into a fire, was assaulted by a man identified by the Associated Press as David Cravens, "an animal rights activist." Skupin was at a function in Columbia, Missouri on June 12, 2001 when Cravens attacked him with pepper spray. Several bystanders, including some children, were also hit, the wire service reported.

PETA, while not denouncing Cravens' attack, quickly made certain to everyone that he was not a PETA associate or member.

Eleven months earlier, in July 2000, *Survivor* producer Mark Burnett had to get a restraining order against a woman identified in news reports as Donna LaPerch. Allegedly, LaPerch was outraged over a *Survivor* episode in which the contestants ate rats, so she sent an e-mail to Burnett stating, "Thankfully, there are people out there who have no qualms about (vengeance) against those who profit and glorify from the deaths of animals."

In late July 2001, a British animal rights extremist named Glynn Harding admitted responsibility for mailing over a dozen letter bombs, three of which caused injuries to people who opened them. Every nail bomb went to an address that was somehow connected with animals and agriculture. They were mailed over a three-month period running from December 2000 to February 2001. One of his victims was blinded in one eye, and another victim – a 6-year-old girl – was left with scars.

These people, and others like them, are enemies of society, lurking quietly within society until they strike, cowardly and covertly, typically under cover of darkness and after taking precautions against having their identities revealed. Unlike a war by one nation against another, animal rights extremists have, much like the Islamic fanatics of al Qaeda, simply declared a war that, for all practical intent, they are waging against humanity.

As President George Bush made clear in the wake of the Sept. 11, 2001 attacks, there can be no middle ground against such a threat. You are either against terrorists, or you are for them.

In the case of animal rights extremism, which manifests itself on many different levels, from relatively harmless nude demonstrations against fur to deliberately harmful arsons, tree spiking, letter bombings and physical assault, it seems only fair to apply the "Newkirk standard" to every one of the offenders and their philosophical supporters. They are all one and the same, whether they commit the crimes, or simply advocate their commission, giving others the motivation to take action.

Just how much closer to such encouragement could someone come than Newkirk, in this statement quoted by the *New York Daily News* in its Dec. 12, 1997 edition: "Would I rather the research lab that tests on animals is reduced to a bunch of cinders? Yes."

The animal rights movement has spawned a crop of domestic, and even international, criminals, large scale and small, and they have collectively accumulated a string of court convictions ranging from simple misdemeanors to state and federal felonies. Its overt connection with the radical environmental campaign leaves no question about the intent, or the intensity, of its advocates.

Property theft or destruction, assault and battery, mailing explosive devices are all practices that are morally and legally wrong. Would it seem reasonable, then, for even the slightest financial support for such activities, or for the people who engage in those unlawful acts, to be tax exempt?

Hate Crimes?

That stated, while it falls within acceptable – though certainly distasteful for many – bounds to acknowledge that people with whom one disagrees still have a right to speak and act in an appropriate and legal way, when does it become unacceptable to provide for such organizations the umbrella protection of tax exemption?

Probably that loss of acceptance comes when one crosses the line into a rather newly-recognized realm of criminal activity, that of the "hate crime." What is a hate crime? That is any crime committed against another based on various criteria that, when boiled down to their lowest common denominator, constitute an act by one person against another or several others based on their race, religion, national origin, skin color, political affiliation and even lifestyle, when one considers that crimes against homosexuals are now commonly considered hate crimes.

But is it a hate crime to harass or attack someone because they eat meat? Is it a hate crime to destroy a meat packing plant or fur farm? Is it a hate crime to physically interfere with hunters engaged in a legal hunting season, or to vandalize their vehicles? Perhaps not under existing statutes, but the fact that many of the extremists who have attacked others did so out of hatred appears irrefutable.

Is it merely an assault to splash real blood or fake blood on someone's fur coat, or is that a hate crime rooted in someone's extremist opposition to the wearing of furs? It may be a crime of hate, but evidently not an official "hate crime" as currently defined. Might it not be appropriate to revisit the hate crime definition? After all, if it is a hate crime to bash a gay man for wearing loud clothing, is it any less an offense to assault someone for wearing a fur?

Hate crimes can be prosecuted at both the state and federal levels, depending upon the individual state statutes. Should perpetrators of crimes against people or property involved in animal research, mink farming, cattle ranching, dairy farming or hunting and fishing, or organizations that encourage such acts without officially coordinating or condoning them, enjoy the status of tax exemption in the process?

Why should there be any difference between any criminal act founded on hatred of lifestyle, philosophy or occupation and a criminal act founded on hatred of one's skin color, religion or national origin?

If the Ku Klux Klan were today to declare itself a 501 (c)(3), and request a tax exempt status while gathering contributions to support various nondescript "program activities," just how would that square with the Internal Revenue

Service?

If a different organization were to have the 501 protection, then turn around and give money to "defense funds" set up for racist or homophobic killers, would not the public outcry be deafening?

Let's consider a hypothetical scenario. In the aftermath of the Oklahoma City bombing, former President Clinton and some people in his administration were very quick to suggest that the crime might have some tenuous connection to conservative talk radio or the gun rights movement. For the sake of argument, let us consider the ramifications if the National Rifle Association's NRA Foundation – itself a tax-exempt entity – were to have provided grants to individuals or organizations that were later revealed to have been involved in criminal acts. Would that not be the catalyst for that organization's downfall, if not the prosecution and imprisonment of its leadership?

The NRA is hardly the most politically correct group on the map, yet it is also a proud organization widely considered to be the "Red Cross of Firearms Safety." It has endured a history of being reviled and viciously stereotyped in editorials, on television shows and even movie screens. Yet the NRA has never in its history advocated a criminal act. You do not hear its leaders advocating the destruction of private or public property at its annual conventions. It is a respectable organization among whose members are, and have been, some remarkable individuals including presidents of the United States, governors, congressmen, doctors, attorneys, police officers, military heroes, sports figures, actors, teachers and journalists. Even with that, the NRA is arguably the most despised organization on the planet, at least by the media elite and far left liberal establishment. What if some reporter discovered the NRA had quietly slipped money to the Timothy McVeigh defense fund?

You can rest assured the news networks and every newspaper editorial page in the country would be screaming hysterically for an immediate investigation, on the level of an inquisition, until punishment was meted out and the organization, itself, were in ruin.

Why then should the same standard of accountability not be applied to People for the Ethical Treatment of Animals? PETA's leaders over the years have given not-so-subtle encouragement to dangerous extremists who just "might" drop a lighted match at a mink farm or feed warehouse. PETA has, over the years, served as a mouthpiece for ALF, whose only apparent purpose is to burglarize and/or destroy private and public property, typically with firebombs. PETA has contributed directly to the defense funds of accused — and eventually convicted — animal rights or eco-terrorists, and on one occasion been caught lying about it.

What separates PETA in terms of accountability — at least in the court of public opinion — from an organization that might have funneled money to Middle Eastern terrorists? Is it so much different to endorse the idea of burning down a research facility in the name of animal rights than it is to nod approval for burning down a Southern Baptist church building because the congregation is African-American?

Where does it stop? At what point does society draw a line and then take sanctions against those who cross it?

Perhaps equally important to consider, at what point does a movement — any movement — having attracted all varieties of individuals who may be more interested in pursuing their own destructive agendas, conclude that it must police its own ranks and divest itself of those whose actions serve more to hurt than support the goals toward which it strives?

Most assuredly, as a society whose cornerstone is freedom, there should be no infringement on the right of people to sincerely, and peacefully (in other words, non-violently), express their disapproval about meat diets or fur-lined garments, or to voice concerns over the treatment of animals at cattle ranches, dairies, laboratories and even veterinary clinics and pet shelters. Such philosophical disagreements fall within the constitutionally protected right of free speech.

But is urging people to not wear fur coats anywhere near the level of suggesting openly that it would be a great thing for someone to torch a dairy, or a college building? Must peaceful protest carry with it the threat – implied or immediate – that there could be criminal force if demands are not met?

The questions seem perfectly clear, and it should not require a college degree, a Congressional investigation, or even a lot of deep thought to provide the answers.

Twelve

DROWNING IN DENIAL
(...While Planning for the Future)

Predicting the future is an endeavor best left to soothsayers and arrogant network news analysts, but if there is a future for the animal rights movement, perhaps it may lie in the message of Joanne Stepaniak, author of eight vegan cookbooks and media coordinator for the North American Vegetarian Society.

She wrote an essay not long ago that seemed as far removed from the usual animal rights drivel that it might almost make one believe that there may be some hope for rationality and reason within the animal rights movement after all. Perhaps Stepaniak's conclusions come from her background in education, sociology and anthropology, areas in which she holds college degrees. Could be her research for the book *Compassionate Living for Healing, Wholeness & Harmony* had some influence on her thinking.

It certainly could not have been the rantings of a Rodney Coronado, Ingrid Newkirk or Alex Pacheco, or their associates, but it could easily be a response to those people.

In her remarkable essay, *Standing in the Fire*, Stepaniak writes: "There is an undercurrent of anger among many vegans and animal activists and, regrettably, it has become one of the central characteristics by which outsiders define us...

155

"Aggression and mean-spiritedness are ugly. They also are cowardly, self-centered, and injurious, especially when they contradict the basic message of a movement. The hostility we have demonstrated toward those with whom we disagree equals and often exceeds the antagonism we have received from them...

"In numerous ways *we* have become our own enemy, because unless we are emotionally mature enough to squelch our resentments, ignore petty differences, and relinquish the egotistical desire to prove ourselves victors over each other, we will never be able to achieve anything of lasting consequence for those we say we care about most. If we are a movement teeming with angry and resentful people, we will be spreading anger, not compassion. It is deluded to think that we simply are dispersing information about animal oppression or raising awareness about compassion if our dealings among ourselves and with others are cloaked in rage....

And she poignantly concludes, "We are standing in the middle of a blaze *we* have set. Unless we learn how extinguish or step outside the flames, we will burn ourselves alive."

Rather out of character for the kind of extremist that seems to have been attracted to PETA, ALF and any number of other animal rights organizations. Stepaniak, if one accepts her message as sincere, is not the skulking anarchist who would covertly firebomb a university research lab or raid a poultry ranch.

Just as likely, and regrettably so, she is not the future leader of the animal rights movement. While her remarks would be considered by any reasonable person to be just the kind of soul-searching required within the animal rights community today, it would appear that the extremists still hold the power, and still determine the course. From all indications, ranging from a continuing, and perhaps increasing, state of denial to the planning of new disruptive strategies, it is, alas, the Ingrid Newkirks and not the Joanne Stepaniaks who appear to be in complete control of the animal rights agenda, and they are adamant that they have done nothing wrong.

In fact, an article published in the June 22, 2002 edition of the *Norfolk Virginian-Pilot* suggested they were in a state of indignant denial. Stung by suggestions in print and on Capitol Hill that PETA and al-Qaeda have much in common, and none too happy about the Center for the Defense of Free Enterprise's request that its tax-exempt status be revoked, PETA threatened lawsuits against its critics.

PETA attorney Jeffrey S. Kerr, quoted in the article, insisted – as he did in his March 2002 letter to Rep. Scott McInnis, chairman of the Congressional subcommittee that held hearings on terrorism – "The whole notion that PETA supports terrorism is false and defamatory. When you use the word 'terror,' look at the terror inflicted on billions of animals in this country every year. That's real terror."

That is also real denial.

Kerr insisted that the attacks on PETA were merely new attempts to smear the organization.

So much for Stepaniak's plea for reason and rational discourse.

Animal Rights Conference 2002

As handily as the animal rights movement, with PETA at the center of its universe, dismisses criticism of its tactics, it most assuredly will dismiss the pleadings of Joanne Stepaniak, if the conduct and content of the 2002 Animal Rights Conference is any indication.

Largely ignored by most news media, the 2002 conference was monitored by a group called Americans for Medical Progress (AMP). Much like the revealing comments published by Dr. James M. Beers about the 2001 conference, the AMP account of the 2002 event revealed much about what animal rights extremists are planning over the horizon. AMP's analysis: "The animal rights movement's leadership is maturing and their organizations are focusing an increasing amount of their resources and energies not on protests and violent actions, but on tools of policy development, litigation, legislation, and education to bring about public acceptance of the animal rights philosophy and agenda."

The short translation: "In your face" will be replaced by "In your lives...increasingly and forever."

According to AMP Vice President Cate Alexander, the group exists in large part because PETA and the animal rights movement exists. She acknowledged that there is no direct contact between AMP and PETA, and that her pro-research organization is more likely to be mentioned – never with flattery – in communiqués from the PCRM, the offshoot of PETA that claims to be an independent animal rights physicians' group.

Perhaps the only sign that PETA and other groups have taken at least some of what Stepaniak wrote to heart was in the AMP's assertion that the in-fighting found at previous conferences seems to have disappeared, though not entirely. Newkirk was back after the previous year's hiatus (she skipped the 2001 conference) to deliver the keynote speech, which, itself, reflected something of a "state of denial" when she insisted to the audience that, "It is our opposition who are the terrorists."

Perhaps to balance Newkirk's apparent resurgence, according to Alexander, ELF's Craig Rosebraugh was nowhere to be seen. Newkirk's return was accompanied by what appeared to be a much larger "presence" and direct influence on the proceeding by PETA staffers.

There were, according to AMP, other developments worthy of continued scrutiny. Veteran animal rights extremist Kim Stallwood, an early career mentor of PETA founder Alex Pacheco, announced the planned development of the "Institute for Animals in Society." A goal of this new "institute" will be to promote the creation of accredited animal rights curricula at colleges and universities so students with animal rights sentiments can "learn social movement politics, learn about the issues, learn about being a more effective advocate (and) learn about our opposition."

This could tie in with a suggestion from PETA's Andrew Butler that colleges and universities might succumb to pressure and stop participating in animal research projects. To accomplish this, animal activists would pressure alumni to stop contributing to their alma maters, or they might attend fundraising events and make embarrassing comments or offer embarrassing toasts.

On the political front, some speakers announced plans to develop grassroots political movements and facilitate networking between the various animal rights groups. Those who had evidently been angry the year before about PETA's media exposure and campaigns appeared to have buried the hatchet, at least for the time being.

Stallwood also briefed the audience about the stages through which any social movement must advance to achieve its ultimate goal. Those states are public education, policy development, legislation, litigation and public acceptance. Quoted by AMP, Stallwood remarked, "We need to understand that while we will change as many people as we can, we will also have to be agents of change in the institutions that make up society."

As discussed previously, that translates to infiltrating institutions and agencies with the goal of affecting their policies. Imagine, for a moment, someone of Alex Pacheco's extremist views one day rising to become the director of a state fish and game agency.

Yet another PETA staffer, Tracy Reiman, offered details on how PETA mounts campaigns against various targets, such as McDonalds and other fast-food chains. AMP detailed eight specific guidelines Reiman listed for would-be activists to follow when staging an action against a specific target.

Meanwhile, Wayne Pacelle with the Humane Society of the United States noted that "Humane USA," an animal rights political action committee, would be spending an estimated $400,000 during the 2002 political campaign season, and eventually plans to have activists in each of the nation's 435 congressional districts.

Yet, with all the discussion about grassroots organization and conducting very public campaigns against specific targets, there was still an undercurrent of support for violent protest as an effective weapon in the war for animal rights. Make no mistake, those who advocate illegal and violent tactics, from burglaries to fire bombings, view this as nothing less than a moral war, and they appear eager as ever to fight that war with fire. That they can easily enlist or encourage anarchists – for whom there may be no genuine "cause" other than having an excuse to destroy someone else's property for the delight of doing it – should give pause to anyone in the meat, fish and poultry industries, fur farming and most assuredly research that involves experiments on live animals.

'Use Violent Tactics'

According to the AMP report, Jerry Vlasak with the Animal Defense League pretty much set the tone for those who advocate crossing the legal line with the following statement: "Every social justice movement has embraced violence and every successful social justice movement has utilized violent tactics to achieve their goals. I don't think it is possible without that. I think we have to quit waiting until everyone is behind us before we embrace new tactics."

Kevin Jonas, the activist from Stop Huntingdon Animal Cruelty (SHAC), also "tried to justify the use of violence as an acceptable tactic," the AMP report went on. He considers violence a cornerstone of the "animal rights arsenal" and he offered what was described as "an impassioned defense" of ALF.

According to the AMP transcript, Jonas, during a speech, asked, "Why shouldn't any one of us think 'it shouldn't be me' taking that brick and shoving it through that window? ...It's not hard. It doesn't take a rocket scientist. You don't need a four year degree to call in a bomb hoax. These are easy things and they are things that save animals."

Yet another account of the 2002 Conference, published in the July 10, 2002 edition of the *New York Post* quoted Capt. Paul Watson, founder and president of the Sea Shepherd Conservation Society (recall that PETA co-founder Pacheco sailed in 1979 aboard the *Sea Shepherd*). According to reporter Ken Moran,'s account, Watson told his audience that if someone ever died from one of his actions, he would consider that "collateral damage."

It is doubtful that such die-hard advocates of the use of violence were swayed much by the pleadings of Ken Shapiro from the Psychologists for the Ethical Treatment of Animals, who cautioned, "violence as a tactic has to be off the map." Would that it were true, but nobody should be surprised at future arsons, burglaries and other "raids" clandestinely perpetrated by individuals using the excuse of animal liberation for their misdeeds.

As if to underscore that point, so-far unidentified animal rights terrorists struck in Seattle, Washington on July 10, 2002 with smoke bombs in two downtown office buildings. The targets were subsidiaries of an insurance company that does business with Huntingdon Life Sciences, and it appeared from the outset that SHAC activists were responsible.

Predictably, spokespersons for SHAC interviewed on two different Seattle radio stations denied direct responsibility for the actions but endorsed and attempted to justify what had been done. The smoke bombs emptied out both office buildings, and did create fear among many employees of both firms, and even people not connected with either business – Marsh Inc. and Guy Carpenter & Company, Inc. – who told local reporters that they were reminded of the Sept. 11 terrorist attack on the World Trade Center's twin towers in New York.

Asked by KVI talk host Kirby Wilbur about his involvement in the animal rights movement, SHAC's Kevin Jonas offered this response: "I think we all have our skill levels and our comfort levels...I volunteer with an above-ground organization. That doesn't mean I don't support underground people who take it a step further."

Recall from Chapter 4 that Jonas (also spelled Kjonass) has in the past called himself a "spokesman" for the ALF. As he had in those days never acknowledge any direct connection with any of the ALF actions he "publicized," Jonas maintained his innocence in connection with the Seattle smoke bombings, and at least in this case, he had an alibi: He was clear across the country when the incident happened.

Yet it is this sort of denial – distancing one's self physically while encouraging and condoning criminal acts – that appears to have become the first rule of order for the more prominent animal rights extremists: Protect *Numero Uno* above all, especially from arrest.

It might be worthy to note at this point that most of those more prominent activists have been arrested and jailed before. It appears quite clear that, while they spare no rhetoric encouraging others to break the law and terrorize people, they have already been in jail and – despite claims to the contrary that they are willing to sacrifice to save the animals – they are not terribly eager to go back to jail again. It is somewhat comparable to the leaders of al-Qaeda and Hezbollah encouraging young Palestinians and Muslim extremists to blow themselves up in homicide bombings, while they, themselves, sit back and wait for the television cameras to record their sound bites for the evening news.

Jonas, at the 2002 Animal Rights Conference, reportedly told his audience, "People have gone, and are going to go, to prison. People have been hurt. People have been sued. People have been deported from countries. People have died and are going to die."

Considering Jonas' demeanor during the Wilbur interview, he is referring to other people. Prison, deportation, litigation and even death; these are all adventures that Jonas obviously would rather not experience on any personal level.

So, when Jonas declared during a fiery speech at the 2002 conference that, "This is a fight that when push comes to shove, I'm ready to push, shove, kick and I'm ready to win," he's just not ready to risk his own neck doing it.

Likewise, fellow SHAC activist and spokesperson Angela Jackson insisted to talk host Dori Monson at rival KIRO-AM that SHAC was not responsible for the Seattle event, but that she sympathized with those responsible.

In both interviews, Jonas and Jackson revealed the strategy that SHAC and other animal rights activists will be using, and which has been hinted at for some time. They compared the crusade for animal rights to the 19th Century battle against slavery, apparently believing this message has more public appeal than simply admitting that some of the more violent animal rights activists are "people haters" or anarchists looking for an excuse to destroy something.

Begging For Infiltrators

Another revelation AMP included in its report on the 2002 Animal Rights Conference was that "Representatives of both PETA and In Defense of Animals (IDA) said that a major component of their anti-research campaigns will remain the infiltration of research facilities."

IDA is apparently "hiring" activists while PETA merely seemed to be encouraging "entrepreneurs" to launch their own efforts then work with PETA in the aftermath for publicity. Here, again, though it is not actually stated in plain language, both groups are recruiting others to do the "dirty work" that could cause individual infiltrators legal problems. Rather than mount their own campaigns, the animal rights leaders are looking for fresh, young bodies to throw on the front lines, while the leaders remain in the rear.

During discussions about infiltration (according to the AMP account supplied to the author by AMP's Alexander) IDA's Matt Rossell stated, "You cannot underestimate the stupidity of our enemy." He repeated that later, adding that the "enemy" – meaning facilities that would unknowingly hire activists – do not conduct very thorough background checks on prospective employees.

If the medical research community ever hopes to prevent the kinds of covert operations that have been conducted ever since Alex Pacheco was a young PETA activist, then it will have to revise and strengthen its hiring process.

The reason for this should be obvious. Not only would this be a defense against infiltration, it might also prevent acts of corporate sabotage. Today's dedicated animal rights infiltrator is someone who will prepare for their undercover work by studying before they apply for a job. Michelle Thew, representing the British Union Against Vivisection, cautioned her audience that they need to know the science. She also urged them to work with one another, even across borders, and to "think globally and act globally."

Getting publicity, especially the positive kind, appears more important to the aging crop of animal rights extremists than it did in the past. For example, PETA's Bruce Friedrich advised his listeners, "Nothing is more important than how our movement is portrayed in the media. And nothing is more important than our movement."

Julie Lewin, founder of the National Institute for Animal Advocacy (NIAA) and president of Animal Advocacy of Connecticut, encouraged her audience to organize and find full-time lobbyists to work the various state legislatures. NIAA was founded "to create a political culture in the animal rights movement and to raise the level of discourse."

Minnesota Sets Example

There is, perhaps, a counter to animal rights terrorism, one that PETA and its allies are unhappy about, and which could – along with denial of tax exempt status to any groups that provide public encouragement and even the slightest degree of financial support for such terrorism – sound the death knell for the animal rights movement as we know it today.

Former Minnesota Gov. Jesse Ventura, who will likely be remembered more prominently as the gravel-voiced, bald-headed, tough-talking ex-Navy SEAL and pro-wrestler who seized the governor's mansion for a single, wild term, will be remembered less fondly and with no amusement whatsoever, by the animal rights front. For it was Ventura who signed into law a state measure that, if followed by other states, will seriously discourage many a would-be animal crusader.

On July 1, 2002, a new anti-terrorism law took effect in Minnesota that increased fines against animal rights activists who destroy research. It was part of the state's enhanced statute against terrorism and clearly places animal rights terrorism on the same level as other types of terrorist acts.

Under Minnesota's statute, there are now stiffer penalties for anyone committing a felony to further terrorism. It is now a felony for anyone to damage or disrupt the operation of a "critical public service."

Animal rights groups who take credit for the actions of vandals could theoretically be held criminally liable for up to three times the value of the damage. They could also face fines of up to $100,000 to compensate for delays in any research damaged or destroyed by such vandalism.

And harshest of all, the Minnesota statute includes a provision that anyone convicted of causing the death of another person while committing a terrorist act could face a first-degree murder conviction with the maximum sentence of life without the possibility of parole.

To combat animal rights terrorists and discourage their acts, other states should pass similar legislation. It would be hard, if not impossible, to find any disagreement with that approach in Seattle following the smoke bomb attack there, which left the downtown area paralyzed, and thousands of workers frightened out of their wits.

Likewise, it will be difficult for animal rights extremists to attack such laws on the grounds that these statutes infringe on their First Amendment rights. The public understands there is no right to destroy or terrorize in the name of some cause, and sentiment now toward any level of terrorism after Sept. 11, 2001 is very low. The overwhelming majority of Americans look upon such actions, and the disingenuous semantics of animal rights leaders to be nothing short of moral bankruptcy.

In the aftermath of the Seattle attack, and in other communities where animal rights extremists are challenged by reporters or talk radio to justify their activities, public sentiment tilts quickly away from such zealots and their causes. The harder that extremists try to sway, or push, the public to adopt their principles, the greater will become the public's resistance. Rather than making more friends, actions that range from laboratory raids to smoke bombs to burglary and arson merely serve to alienate a growing segment of the population.

One can only caution the more aggressive animal rights extremists to pay heed to one of their own, Michael Budkie, founder of Stop Animal Exploitation Now and co-founder of the National Activists Network. During the discussion at the 2002 Animal Rights Conference about the use of violence as a tactic, Budkie warned his audience that violence in the name of animal rights convinces many Americans that "we're a bunch of crazies."

Not All Is Well

The claim that all is well within the animal rights community seems more than just a bit off the mark, as there appears to be a growing concern that feminists involved in the movement are trying to pursue their own agenda. On the other hand, they may not really be involved in the movement at all, but are simply another interest group attracted to a gathering of presumably like-minded individuals and organizations, all with a common axe to grind against what they consider an overall unjust society.

Whatever the case, the aftermath of an incident at the conference has created more than just a ripple in the animal rights community.

One attendee wrote in an e-mail posted to the conference's internet "Memories Board" that, "racism and sexism were rampant. Women were violated and betrayed by the men running the show. Getting from opening day through the awards banquet was running a gauntlet reminiscent of Tailhook…"

In response, another e-mail – written by a woman in attendance – stated, "I have deep concerns with the animal right – feminist (sic) being part of the movement because they have distracted from our mission and vision of animal liberation and have turned it into their own agenda…"

All of this revolves around a small tempest that erupted during the awards banquet, when master of ceremonies Howard Lyman, a "born-again" animal rights activist who used to be a rancher, made some remarks considered politically incorrect, at least by some members of the audience.

Lyman, introducing Miss World USA Natasha Allas – an advocate of animal rights –reportedly observed, "There have been a number of speakers at this conference who have alluded to the shape of the movement…I would like to introduce you as the ideal shape of the movement." He subsequently made another reference to Miss Allas' "shape" and in response, over 20 people in the audience got up in a huff and walked out.

Complicating the matter rather than helping to calm things, Conference Chairman Alex Hershaft with the International Vegetarian Union (and yet another activist who, on the IVU website, is credited with launching the animal rights movement in America) took the stage and lamely joked, "I want to assure everybody that all rumors to the effect that the MC is a sexist pig are totally unfounded. He is not. He adores his wife and he adores women."

This sort of remark makes feminists livid, and those feminists remaining in the audience disrupted the event, loudly criticizing Lyman and insisting that sexism has no place in the animal rights movement.

The following day, an anti-sexism petition sponsored by Barbara Chang – who alleged there was a "misogynistic atmosphere" at the conference – was circulated as she called for a feminist boycott of the next year's event.

Chang, quoted in a CNSNews.com article, stated, "We will continue to fight for the animals, but we can no longer do it with this organization or the men who dominated the conference."

As if to fulfill her wish, Hershaft banned Chang from the 2003 conference. In what can only be considered a bit of heavy irony, Hershaft made some statements that, in careful analysis, might easily be applied to the entire animal rights movement by organizations and individuals it has targeted.

Calling the banquet disruption "a deliberate act of self-indulgence," Hershaft accused the feminists of attending the conference, "to just sit there and wait and listen and look for opportunities to jump in."

Whether there will be any long-term ripples in the animal rights movement over the feminist flap remains to be seen. Yet this incident demonstrates that even within the animal rights community, there is more than one agenda, and some nasty disagreement.

That may not bode well for the future of animal rights, as history has demonstrated time and again that extremists do not long work well with one another.

STRIKING A DELICATE BALANCE

Defending freedom of speech and thought is one of the cornerstones of that foundation which has made America a land where liberty is not just a word on paper, but a principle that binds our social fabric.

While we are a nation of liberty where diverse viewpoints are not simply tolerated but encouraged, we are also a nation of laws. Among those laws are statutes that prohibit arson, burglary, vandalism, theft, other forms of property destruction and criminal assault. It is the right of any group to redress their grievances in a peaceful manner, as provided for and protected by, the Constitution's Bill of Rights. It is not the right of any group to terrorize, harass or intimidate others in pursuit of a goal or, more insidiously, to criminally coerce anyone into accepting a lifestyle with which they disagree. There is even less a "right" for anarchists with no real issue or purpose to wantonly destroy another person's property and livelihood, and later try to justify their empty viciousness by hiding behind a shield of animal "rights."

There is a vast moral, if not legal, gray area into which the likes of People for the Ethical Treatment of Animals have found undeserved and unearned security. This is the realm in which PETA argues its innocence because its leaders merely encourage and give tacit endorsement to the criminal acts of others, while claiming no personal responsibility.

Of course, there remains considerable skepticism about where PETA draws its own line – a line that seems to conveniently shift depending upon the circumstances and the venue – and whether its leaders are much more involved in this campaign of domestic terror than they would publicly acknowledge. There are the legitimate questions about convicted animal rights terrorist Rodney Coronado's connection to PETA founders Ingrid Newkirk and Alex Pacheco, and his Federal Express shipments to her following the Michigan State University attack. Likewise, questions about PETA's financial contributions to Coronado and others charged, and later convicted, of animal rights terrorist actions most be answered plausibly. The Coronado case merely scratches the surface of potential collusion, a potential that begs thorough investigation.

It cannot be overlooked that Newkirk and her colleagues at PETA have been arrested on occasion for various misdemeanors involving animal rights or anti-fur protests.

In a court of law, where clever attorneys can debate the legal technicalities and argue semantics, individuals and organizations frequently get away with this sort of association and relatively petty activity.

It is a different story in the court of public opinion, where intelligent people recognize the differences between right and wrong are not divided by a thin line, but by the deep chasm that always separates good from evil.

PETA's longtime admitted association as a public relations mouthpiece for the terrorist Animal Liberation Front is beyond the point for mere skepticism and it most no longer be condoned. Only an intense investigation will exonerate these people of suspicion, or hold them accountable, either as accessories or as participants in specific criminal acts.

There are questions for philanthropists who contribute to PETA and who may not be aware that PETA in turn may use those contributions to fund other entities and activities which they do not approve. Whether their contributions ultimately go to an organization such as the Physicians Committee for Responsible Medicine or the questionable Foundation to Support Animal Protection, or wind up in the bank account of a convicted domestic terrorist, one must be reminded of the public reaction when campaign contributions to the late President Richard M. Nixon found their way into the bank account of a Watergate burglar.

On the other hand, there may be some legitimate question about whether some of these benefactors actually know, or at least hope, their money may ultimately go to support such animal rights terrorist actions. After all, people like Rodney Coronado need some sort of financing to travel around the country and spread their brand of terrorism. Where has that money come from?

Balanced against all of this is the tolerance that all of society must have for the rights and beliefs of people who are truly committed, in a non-violent way, to humane treatment for animals. No right-thinking human being would condone deliberately cruel and abusive treatment of animals, without some "greater good" benefit for society, such as a cure for cancer or heart disease.

Are there sanctions that could be taken to assure that animal rights terrorism is not underwritten by well-meaning benefactors, much less the general public?

One reasonable step would be to strip the provocateurs of any ability to raise money as tax exempt entities. Society should not subsidize the encouragement of domestic terrorism that fronts itself as concern for the welfare of animals. In cases where tax exempt organizations openly or surreptitiously provide money as payments, grants or contributions to such terrorists, legal sanctions must be taken.

When leaders of tax exempt organizations openly advocate or even "strongly suggest" taking so-called "direct action" on the scale of burglary, vandalism or arson against companies or institutions, they should be held accountable to the same degree that someone would be prosecuted for inciting a riot or organizing a mob that gets out of control. This is far different than organizing a boycott or even peacefully picketing outside a store, restaurant, public institution or private business.

State fish and wildlife agencies must be encouraged by outdoorsmen and women to aggressively enforce their laws against hunter harassment. For too long, state agencies have handled offenders with the proverbial kid gloves approach. Individuals who harass and intimidate hunters, especially juveniles, should be arrested and prosecuted, thus putting on notice other would-be offenders that there is more at risk than simply being told repeatedly by a game warden to leave an area.

If such harassment occurs on federal land, then federal officers must enforce the Recreational Hunting Safety and Preservation Act of 1994 (16 U.S.C. §§ 5201-5207) that was passed as part of the Clinton Crime Control Act in September of that year.

Hunters especially should encourage their state legislators to strengthen these laws, and to pressure wildlife agencies to enforce them.

Parents must pay more attention to the curriculum their youngsters learn in public schools. If there are presentations regarding animal "rights," then school administrations must be required to offer equal exposure to farming, breeding, hunting and other consumptive uses of livestock and wildlife and their positive benefits for society.

School boards should be encouraged to review educational texts and materials, and supplementary materials introduced by teachers at the classroom level, to assure that these materials are balanced and accurate.

We can support research and the institutions that conduct it, while also supporting enforcement of rules that regulate research and the researchers.

Consumers should support businesses that are unfairly and arbitrarily targeted by animal rights protesters. Businesses and their customers should be encouraged to prosecute protesters for harassment or assault, should the situation arise and circumstances warrant it.

The time has long since passed in which business, consumers, hunters, anglers, research facilities and their employees can "turn the other cheek" when dealing with the animal rights community. Society's passiveness and permissiveness has encouraged more aggressive behavior by such groups.

PETA and like-minded extremist groups and individuals have risen to prominence by taking, and encouraging, actions that span the scale of legality and acceptability, all in the name of animal "rights."

Along the way, they have forgotten or deliberately ignored the fact that it is people who have rights. Pretending or imagining otherwise does not make it so, and committing or encouraging terrorist acts assures that it never will.

REFERENCES

Books

Ron Arnold, *Undue Influence*, Free Enterprise Press, Bellevue, Washington, 1999

Ron Arnold and Alan Gottlieb, *Trashing the Economy: How Runaway Environmentalism is Wrecking America*, Second Edition, Free Enterprise Press, Bellevue, Washington, 1994

Ron Arnold, *EcoTerror: The Violent Agenda To Save Nature – The World of the Unabomber*, Free Enterprise Press, Bellevue, Washington, 1997

Kathleen Marquardt, Hervert M. Levine and Mark LaRochelle, *Animal Scam: The Beastly Abuse of Human Rights*, Regnery Gateway, Chicago, 1993

News Articles and Publications

Ananova, *Shock animal rights advert banned from cinemas*, May 29, 2002

Associated Press, *PETA Calls Attacks a New Breed of McCarthyism*, March 16, 2002

Associated Press, *PETA files complaint over treatment of UNC lab rats*, May 2, 2002

Shannon Brescher, *Pease '00 Arrested for Burglary*, Cornell Daily Sun, Feb. 8, 2002

Brian Carnell, *Ongoing Investigation of University of Minnesota ALF Action*, AnimalRights.Net, July 1999

Brian Carnell, *Did SHAC Illegally Transfer Funds from American Charity to British Protesters?* Animal Rights.Net, Jan. 9, 2002

177

Brian Carnell, *ALF Takes Credit for Fire at Indiana Poultry Distributor*, Animal Rights.Net, May 30, 2002

Brian Carnell, *Dateline Covers the Howard Baker Controversy*, Animal Rights.Net, May 30, 2001

Brian Carnell, *PETA and Undercover Operative Sued by Veterinarian*, Animal Rights.Net, Nov. 27, 2000

Brian Carnell, *Supreme Court Agrees to Hear RICO Lawsuit Appeal*, Animal Rights.Net, April 22, 2002

Brian Carnell, *Quotes From Animal Rights Activists*, Animal Rights.Net, May 14, 2000

Brian Carnell, *PETA protester charged with arson*, Animal Rights.Net, July 5, 1999

Brian Carnell, *PETA Puts Supporter of Violence on Its Payroll*, Animal Rights.Net, May 29, 2002

Elisabeth Carnell, *Animal Rights Groups Go Too Far*, AnimalRights.net, May 14, 2000

Matthew Cella, *PETA's charity status questioned*, The Washington Times, March 5, 2002

Peter Conradi, *Fortuyn killer linked to earlier death*, Sunday Times of London, May 12, 2002

ConsumerFreedom.com, Activist Cash

Bryan Denson and James Long, *Ideologues drive the violence*, Portland Oregonian, Sept. 27, 1999

Tom DeWeese, *Animal Rights Terrorists Gather to Plot Havoc*, CNSNews.com, June 21, 2001

Earth Liberation Front, *Setting Fires With Electrical Timers*, May 2001

Sarah Foster, *Eco-group violated tax laws?* WorldNetDaily.com, Feb. 17, 2002

Stefan C. Friedman, *The PETA-ELF Connection*, New York Post, March 7, 2002

Candace Heckman, *Zoo's treatment of elephants is too harsh, PETA says*, Seattle Post-Intelligencer, July 3, 2002

William T. Jarvis, Ph.D., *Physician's Committee For Responsible Medicine*, National Council Against Health Fraud newsletter, Jan. 15, 2001

Brad Knickerbocker, *Animal Activists Get Violent*, Christian Science Monitor, Aug. 29, 1997

Gina Kolata, *Tough Tactics in Battle Over Animals in the Lab*, New York Times, March 24, 1998

John D. Lawley, *Are There Grounds for the Revocation of PETA's Tax-Exempt Status? An Examination of the Financial Relationship Between PETA and Eco-Terrorism*, April 2002

Jack Lessenberry, *Activist Devotes Life to Animal Rights*, Toledo Blade, June 24, 2001

John Fulton Lewis, *Growing Suspicion: Are We Facing a 'Blofeld' Threat?* Alliance For America, April 10, 2001

David Martosko, *Animal Rights Fanatics: Doctor Dolittle gone bad*, Seattle Times, July 15, 2002

Mitchell Maddux, *Secret Agent for Animals Draws Veterinarian's Suit*, The Record (Bergen County, NJ), Nov. 24, 2000

Steven Milloy, *The Federal DA's Subversive Son*, New York Post, March 15, 2002

Marc Morano, *Animal 'Rights' Zealot: Christianity Harmful; Infanticide OK*, CNSNews.com, July 2, 2002

Marc Morano, *Feminists Battle 'Animal Rights' Activities Over Alleged Sexism*, CNSNews.com, July 16, 2002

Gene Mueller, *PETA officials collide with deer*, The Washington Times, March 10, 2002

Ingrid Newkirk, *PETA 'Terra-ists'*, CNSNews.com, Nov. 5, 2001

No Compromise, Issue 15, Page 15.

Gretchen Randall, *Whistleblowers: FWS cover-up includes intimidation and obstruction of justice*, January 2000

Ray Ring, *Unarmed but dangerous critics close in on hunting*, High Country News, Dec. 11, 1995

John Rossomando, *Tax Documents Link Medical Group To Animal Rights Movement*, CNSNews.com

Christopher Ruddy, *White House Tried to Use Gun Tax to Ban Hunting*, NewsMax.com, July 3, 2000

Michael Satchell, *Terrorize people, save animals*, USNews.com, April 8, 2002

Sentence in activist's pie incident, Las Vegas Review Journal, Dec. 5, 2000

Judi Sokolowski, *PETA could lose nonprofit status, Animal-rights organization gave money to group on FBI's 'terrorist' list*, Spokane Spokesman Review, May 28, 2002

Michael Standaert, *Fortuyn lost life over fur farming*, The Washington Times, May 20, 2002

Joanne Stepaniak, *Standing in the Fire*, Vegsource.com

Steward Truelsen, *PETA Exposed on Eco-terrorism*, The Voice of Agriculture, March 11, 2002

Daniel Walsh, *E. Brunswick veterinarian to appeal July conviction*, The Sentinel, March 24, 2000

Will Woodard, *On Campus, Animal Rights vs. Animal Research*, The Washington Post, Nov. 5, 1999

Norma Bennett Woolf, *PETA sued*, NAIA Online, July-August 1997

Norma Bennett Woolf, *Veterinarian wins appeal; PETA charges thrown out*, NAIA Online, July 2000

Contact Organizations

Center for Consumer Freedom
P.O. Box 27414
Washington, DC 20038

Center for the Defense of Free Enterprise
Liberty Park / 12500 N.E. Tenth Place
Bellevue, WA 98005

Ducks Unlimited
One Waterfowl Way
Memphis, TN 38120

Foundation for North American Wild Sheep
720 Allen Ave.
Cody, WY 82414

Mule Deer Foundation
1005 Terminal Way, Suite 170
Reno, Nevada 89502

National Wild Turkey Federation
Post Office Box 530
Edgefield, SC 29824-1510

New Mexico Center for Wildlife Law
University of New Mexico School of Law
1117 Stanford NE, Albuquerque, NM 87131
(505) 277-5006

Pheasants Forever
1783 Buerkle Circle
St. Paul, Minnesota 55110

Quail Unlimited National Headquarters
31 Quail Run or P. O. Box 610
Edgefield, South Carolina 29824

Rocky Mountain Elk Foundation
2291 W Broadway
P.O. Box 8249
Missoula, MT 59807

Ruffed Grouse Society
451 McCormick Rd.
Coraopolis, PA 15108

U.S. Sportsmen's Alliance
801 Kingsmill Parkway
Columbus, OH 43229-1137

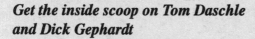